The End of an Era

Diverse Thoughts from 100+ Years of Living

JOHN H. MANHOLD

NEWMAN SPRINGS PUBLISHING
320 Broad Street
Red Bank, NJ 07701

First originally published by Newman Springs Publishing 2021

ISBN 978-1-63692-563-9 (Paperback)
ISBN 978-1-63692-564-6 (Digital)

Printed in the United States of America

To Enriqueta Manhold
My beautiful, intelligent, constant
companion for the last fifty years.

CONTENTS

Introduction...7

Chapter 1   Beginning Years 13
Chapter 2   Graduate Education and Wars 21
Chapter 3   Serendipity Begins in Earnest 32
Chapter 4   Teaching...38
Chapter 5   Investigative Activities 45
Chapter 6   Writing...55
Chapter 7   Sculpture 79
Chapter 8   The Joys and Other Aspects of
             Owning Boats 85
Chapter 9   Golf and Associated Activities.............97
Chapter 10   Shooting Sports................................104
Chapter 11   Some "Different" Trips 111
Chapter 12   Conclusion....................................119

Closing Remarks 131
About the Author.......................................143
Image Gallery..145

INTRODUCTION

A few questions with respect to this year of 2021.

How often have you entered a store where help purportedly is expected, only to be ignored by workers engaged in continuing conversation, and if attention ultimately is provided, to be informed, "Probably down there in aisle X somewhere" (where aisle X often is Y, Z, or other)?

Or perhaps told, "That's not my department, so I can't help you"?

What about attempting to gain information over the telephone where the same quote is accompanied by a reference to one number or person after another? And that is only *if* you even have been able to reach a person rather than the AI chip that can provide only the material with which it has been programmed. And heaven help you if your question is beyond its programmed knowledge.

The narrowly missed automobile accident because of a driver's urgency to get somewhere but still must attempt to text or engage in a telephone conversation?

How frequently do you encounter empathy or understanding of a problem? Instead, is your boss or other "uncaring" person too occupied to even hear what you are saying?

Or if the person listens, how much is he/she really hearing? The last study of attention span of humans I found was 8.1 seconds, which is comparable to that reported of a goldfish.

Have you noticed how rapidly advertisements change on TV?

How rapidly people speak these days?

When answering the phone, you immediately are addressed by a recorded message?

What has happened to loyalty? Whom do you really believe you personally can trust?

But enough. Dependence upon machines, computers, and artificial intelligence is our way of life. Its pace and the quantity of material required to be gathered and stored has grown far beyond present abilities. Regrettably, no choice exists but to continue ruining the world while opening our lives to any and every one because no computer made to date is immune to hacking.

It also depicts a life far different from mine, which began a few months after the end of World War I. An era of total upheaval in the mores of society was occurring that escalated to almost unimagined levels in communication, transportation, housing, clothing, morals, matters of entertainment, patterns of thought—everything.

The 1919–2021 period of change has been of sufficient magnitude even to be equated with the now almost forgotten Renaissance. Amusingly perhaps, my unusual, highly varied life activities have been suggested as comparable to such an experience and often accompanied with suggestions—actual pressure—to publish them.

Until now, I have refused. Producing another exercise in self-serving egocentricity that few other than family and a few acquaintances might like to read always has seemed gauche. I have not acquired any status as a celebrated professional athlete, revered statesman, honored warrior, or even received extensive media coverage as a celebrated stage or cinematic performer. I have gained a certain level of recognition in several areas—scientific research as a professor, lecturer and consultant, sculptor, author; earned USCG captain and master's papers; received some national and international sport's awards; and served in WWII and the Korean conflict. Many garnered invitations (as well as travelling simply for fun) throughout the United States, much of Europe, the Middle East, parts of the Near East, India, and Latin American countries and with invitations even from Russia, India, and the Far East. Granted, an unusually eclectic and inter-relating mixture of world travels, frequently on someone else's buck; dining; playing golf; shooting; boating; teaching; writing; experimenting with wound healing and other mostly so-called psychosomatic entities, much of which was accomplished when a mind-body relationship had only just been introduced; lecturing and consulting worldwide; and even some time spent in summer stock as well as with declared "celebrities" and even time spent in a couple of wars.

So as time passed, remarks made in social gatherings gradually began to bring forth even more suggestions that I acquiesce even though it is a well-known fact that all old guys have abundant stories, some of which occasionally may make the listener wonder a little with respect to fact versus fiction. But the actual decision to begin a memoir resulted from a casual conversation with a young intern. He said, "Little really new is left to accomplish. In your day, there was so much to discover, and you were free to do what you wanted to do. It also was easier to meet significant people." Although quite negative and only partially true, I began to think about the remarks. Fundamentally, they contain much truth ranging from the perhaps amusingly structured manner of dress—boys wore knickers until the age of twelve or thirteen when they could "graduate to wearing long pants"—to the many serious restrictions that will appear in appropriate ensuing sections. A few examples of the discoveries and opportunities the young intern referred:

- Radio: general ownership of radios did not exist in the early post-WWI days. My father built our first crystal set.
- TV: attended one of the early premanufacture trial television telecasts as my father's guest, viewed from Strong Auditorium as telecast from nearby Murray Hall on the University of Rochester campus.
- Jet flight, Internet, DNA, RNA, cloning, and more.
- Opportunities: Meeting, conversing, and spending time with numerous "celebrities" as will be recalled in appropriate chapters. Of particular interest meeting Albert Einstein and the electrical "genius" Charles Proteus Steinmetz (with later the most gratifying but totally humbling experience of being included in, at that time before vanity publishing reared its ugly head, the highly prestigious Marquis *World Who's Who in Science from Antiquity to the Present*).

But obviously, the century's changes overall have been accumulating for millennia. Only the pace has accelerated and at a pace even faster than during the Industrial Revolution. The past one hundred years had moved from a time when a man's handshake was binding, and a resident of the then *United* States of America was free to indulge in and could attain top-level accomplishments in any number of fields to an era exhibiting differences upon which we shall comment.

Consequently, the intention here is to describe my serendipitous journey in an obvious and/or easily verifiable manner as it occurred with observations on the era differences. And it will offer impressions gained through these years spent with many people of different—or possibly similar but somehow "different"—mores as they change with time. Also, I should like to impart some of the insight (?) gained that could offer takeaway thoughts for others.

And a tangentially pertinent note for the increasing number of business travelers: One becomes astutely aware that only so much time is spent in the actual performance of these matters. In the time remaining, one usually explores and looks for entertainment. If not being particularly inclined to any level of promiscuity, it seemed most appropriate to attempt to discover another person who enjoys the same.

After a couple of misfires, I was able to find such a person—Enriqueta, to whom this book is dedicated—with whom to enjoy the serendipitous journey.

But to conclude: Regrettably, there is a paucity of interest in the past. Few read history with the lessons that it teaches, and even historical novels are passé. The following material sets forth a contrasting picture between the 1900s and the present century. It is one man's story set forth in my words as the events are remembered and written, set with obvious and/or referenced substantiation. The prospective reader can decide whether he/she wants to proceed. If "this is not your thing," please pass by and get a book in the genre you enjoy.

CHAPTER 1
Beginning Years

Quite a number of years ago, I received a copy of a book that I assume was sent to me at the request of my cousin Gerald, who was quite interested in genealogy. Parenthetically, Manhold family member contacts always have been sporadic and/or nonexistent—no rancor, no interfamily problems, just a seeming disinterest. For whatever reason, we both had been somewhat closer to our grandfather, a graduate of the *Kriegsakademie* or Prussian War College, from whom we each had a couple of medals awarded to him during the Franco-Prussian War. The book *The World Book of Manholds* (Hilbert's Family Heritage Publishers) stated it "is not connected in any particular Manhold family and represents a compilation of public information." Gerry is listed correctly while in New Jersey, as is another cousin, Earl and his wife, in Florida, although this was their summer home until retiring from CEO of a well-known candy company. In total, 267 Manholds—fifty-three in the US; three, Great Britain; 208, Germany; three, Switzerland; and three, Italy—were reported. Which begs the question about the worth of services of this type. Several people I know, including myself, are not included.

Accompanying the book, however, was another enclosure containing a letter in German with a note written on the other side in English:

> This letter was carried in the breast pocket of my father, Karl Manhold, in the war of 1870 at Alsace Lorraine, France—the bullet struck him and saved his life due to this letter he wore in his breast pocket over his heart. The hole in the letter, marked by arrow, was where the bullet was stopped from entering his heart.

It is signed by my father's sister Elfrieda Manhold Alison, Rochester, New York. A small hole is marked with an arrow. The paper is some type of somewhat heavier parchment and, I assume, was carried in some sort of metallic or heavy leather container. The size of the hole resembles a shell fragment rather than a bullet and would seem logical, as similar occurrences have been reported of a relatively spent projectile being stopped in a similar manner. The story of the family's move from Germany to the US also is unusual but really irrelevant to this volume.

My early years before entering college were, for the most part, spent similarly to others of my generation. Many encountered various degrees of privation. The stock market collapsed in 1929, and the country entered the Great Depression, from which it still was attempting to recover years later. I was ten years old when it began and more fortunate than most in that my father was an electrical engineer with Eastman Kodak Company, at that time and for many years the largest employer in the city of Rochester, New York. The sordid details of that era are exactly as bad as has been described at length in articles, books, and cinematic productions.

Perhaps century-wise, the most outstanding picture of the depression was the stark contrast between the thought processes of those men and today's workers. The government did *not* supply food stamps, social security, health insurance, or any other means of support for the unemployed. The man of the time needed to work for these necessities, although some necessities were dispensed at the mobile kitchen that always had excessively long waiting lines. But even more pressing were the mores of the time, a matter of self-respect and the reason why PhDs could be found in relatively large supply among the Civilian Conservation Corps (CCC) when it finally was established to repair roads and bridges and other manual labor projects to restore the country's infrastructure. What about the mindset of today's "worker" and the many documented cases of persons preferring to live on the largesse provided by various governmental agencies rather than obtain jobs that are available?

But then again, we can mention a couple of amusing personal reminiscences about the early parts of those times. You could buy an ice cream "big cone" for a nickel. The ice cream was contained in a wrapper that was opened and set within the cone. Its size, three and a half inches high, three inches across the top, tapering down to fit properly within the standard cone opening. The second is that I was able to run a small muskrat trapline in the marshland of the Genesee River, which was a short distance from our home.

Trapped, cleaned, and prepared to sell, each skin sold for seventy-five cents, a lot of money for a kid just teetering on the brink of his teens.

A little later, as things began to pick up, I found a summer vacation job with Abbot, who opened the first frozen custard stand in Rochester, New York. It occupied one of a series of stands of various products along Lake Avenue, which terminated just before the lake with a huge parking lot for Rochesterians and visitors going to the beach to swim. The stand was a two-man operation and started with vanilla custard only that was dipped from a tub into which the product was deposited as it was generated from the machine. Later, he added chocolate. My job was to arrive around 3:30 in the afternoon, receive delivery of the day's ice delivered in three-hundred-pound blocks, and move them by myself into the refrigerator. We opened at 5:00 when my main job began of scooping custard cones for the fast-developing line of customers that on hot summer nights could extend until one and even two in the morning.

Some twenty years ago, I was attending a reunion at the university and took Kit down to see the lake. The stand was still there, and she was able to get a frozen custard served by one of his grandchildren. Since then, I understand it has expanded to several locations.

Other summer and vacation jobs also began to open. I packed hams for Armour & Company on Easter and Christmas vacations and worked in the cine processing division of Kodak, where I chose the 12:00-p.m.-to-8:00-a.m. shift because it paid twenty-six dollars per week versus twenty-four dollars working four to twelve and just twenty-two dollars for 8:00 a.m. to 4:00 p.m.

Perhaps more interesting notes for members of today's more recent generations, we did not have Little League or other subsidized sports established and ruled by parent coaches or individuals hired by them. If not a school-sponsored sport, we attempted to gather enough guys from the neighborhood to play baseball, football, or other "team" sport. If no more than four could be rounded up, the game probably was "One-a-Cat," where there's a batter, catcher, and pitcher, with the fourth member the only person to cover the infield and outfield. When the batter finally was "out," the rotation was the fielder became pitcher, the pitcher the catcher, the catcher the batter, and the hitter moved to the field. Another game was duck on a rock, where a player placed an empty tin can, easily obtainable from any home refuse bin, on a particular selected rock (usually the one that otherwise served as home base for baseball) in the empty field used for the group activities, and defend it against attack by others who attempted to knock it from its position.

Of possible additional interest to those born later in the century and beyond: My father, like many of the generation, enjoyed hunting and fishing. He introduced me to these sports, and I accompanied him on trips to Lake Erie to catch walleyed pike and to Canada to catch muskellunge, a very large fighting fish that is coveted by anglers. Various other places were visited to camp out while hunting deer, bear, ducks, geese, and more. I downed my first deer at the age of twelve in the Allagash River country of Northern Maine and my first ducks the same year in the Montezuma Swamp in New York State. My rifle was a lever action Winchester .45 caliber short carbine or "bush gun," a model whose manufacture was discontinued two or three years later. The shotgun was a single-shot, twenty-gauge model Winchester that has no registration number in that it was manufactured before all firearms were required to be numbered. Both weapons still are in my possession and in good working order.

A note of interest on the Maine location is that Maine's North Woods is quite unlike the rest of the northeast that is heavily visited. Instead, it still is so little visited that there has been almost no change since the nineteenth century. Thus, the remote area has become a canoeist's Mecca. Another is with respect to the name Montezuma Swamp for a location in the Finger Lakes region of New York State. A man by the name of Peter Clark, in some manner impressed with Aztec emperor Montezuma in Mexico City, applied the name to his hilltop home, and the marsh, village, and surrounding area eventually assumed the name. The ponds and associated areas where we had gone duck gunning for years no longer were available after 1938 when it was designated a wildlife sanctuary—the year I began college, incidentally.

In our second year of high school, we acquired a new English teacher, Walter Enright. He had been a successful Broadway play director who had decided a teaching position would provide more stability because of the uncertainties of the profession and his need to take care of his ailing widowed mother. He also initiated a theater group, which I found fascinating, and seemed to exhibit some acting ability. He also directed productions in a nearby summer stock theater that became increasingly prominent in the following years. I was fortunate enough to gain parts in a couple of productions, including the lead role of Captain

Stanhope (originally played by a young Lawrence Olivier) in English playwright R. C. Sherriff's 1928 wartime play *Journey's End*.

These thespian activities for the next few years provided fascinating contact with prominent actors of the time such as William Powell, Kay Francis, and Myrna Loy, with a short stint at the Ogunquit (Maine) Playhouse that opened originally in a renovated garage in 1933 before prominent theater persons Walter and Maude Hartwig moved it into town during the general expansion movement of these small entertainment facilities.

During high school and early college days, I also tried baseball, where I was used only as a pinch hitter; basketball, where I was too short; soccer, where I was the goalie (we had no football in high school); football as a quarterback, which lasted until injuries intervened; and track, where I did not fit anywhere. In wrestling and boxing, I fared better, and I thoroughly enjoyed saber fencing in a group instructed by a professional in downtown Rochester, whose name I no longer recall.

College attendance was a no-brainer. Money still was tight. The University of Rochester had an excellent reputation. I could still live at home. I was involved with the girl I wanted to marry, who also entered the same school. My major? Having become a somewhat voracious reader through the years, I had become interested in "research," but as many other college students with no specific goal in mind, I majored in the catchall premed studies but added a second in Elizabethan and seventeenth-century poets because I was fascinated with the language.

Another incident: The course in Shakespeare was taught by Professor Curtis, who greatly valued the fact that he had been one of the more favored students of Kittredge, the onetime highest authority on "The Bard." In this favored position, Curtis believed himself to be an authority on most writers of the century. I won a discussion convincing him that I was correct in my assessment of two of Spencer's poems.

In my third year in college, Harvard School of Dental Medicine announced an unheard-of progressive move of initiating a six-year program to award degrees in both medicine and dentistry. As the first hesitant step in attempting to progress beyond the dental—and to a large extent medical—profession's long-existing reactionary attitude toward change, the class of '44 would be "the transitional one" in dental/medical education. I completed my application, was accepted, and headed to Boston.

CHAPTER 2
Graduate Education and Wars

Harvard's first hesitant step in defying tradition began with identical basic science instruction taught jointly to the medical/dental students. A most important step considering what transpired as time progressed. Reactionary pressure began almost immediately and grew, perhaps not surprisingly, to significant levels when both dental and medical central administrators could not remove themselves from their long-standing reactionary attitudes. Upon completion of all basic science courses at the end of the second year, the new program died. The university recanted and offered a choice to continue toward the DMD *or* reapply and begin again to progress toward an MD. Fortunately, my completion of the basic medical studies had been validated by the medical and dental deans, and the University of Rochester granted me my undergraduate degree with the class of 1941.

My decision was another obvious no-brainer. I had married my college girlfriend, Vivian Weyraugh, against my father's wishes. So married with no source of support, WWII imminent and other uncertainties of the future, repetition of two years was unconscionable. Our ensuing life was somewhat difficult in spots but also fascinating in that it provided for the examination of unexpected "talents" as well as the development of others that already had benefited from initial experimentation. Money was short, and jobs included table waiter, short-order cook, and yard work during the summer in Harvard Square. While working out in the school's gym, I was approached with a question as to if I wanted to make fifty dollars that night. My answer: "Who would I have to kill?" To put that amount of money into perspective, my tuition for the entire year at that time was four hundred dollars. Parenthetically, I won by knockout in the second round, which led to further invitations with higher payoffs, and this leads to another amusing story pertinent later. Also acquired was a "good job" as a fill-in line cook at the Buckminster Hotel in Kenmore Square (now, I believe a dormitory for Boston university). Vivian was an attractive, outgoing person whose mother was from Aberdeen, Scotland and a distant relative to the Queen (who was a commoner). She obtained a secretarial position at Harvard that again offers an aside.

She became friends with the daughter of Joe Kennedy's partner in the Merchandise Mart in Chicago, who, at that time, I understood, was an important figure in movie distribution on the east coast. The two gals ate lunch regularly at a favorite place in Cambridge, where they were joined occasionally by Eunice Kennedy, who occasionally was saddled with little Teddy. I frequently joined them for lunch, found Eunice pleasant, Teddy as obnoxious as a kid as he was later in life, and Jack joined us on one occasion when on leave. He was a pleasant guy.

Life was a little hectic but fun. World War II began not too long thereafter; our schooling was accelerated, and we were inducted as student officers and graduated early to become officers in the US Navy or Army Reserve on active duty, as we had chosen. Viv and I headed for Bainbridge, Maryland, NTS with more training in nearby army facilities, a stint aboard the Billy Mitchel troop carrier, and a little marine training. My WWII service lasted from May 4, 1944, to April 24, 1946. The war ended, and we headed back to Boston, but I stayed on active reserve. Because my original intention in entering the dual degree program was a desire to pursue a career in research, upon release from active duty and thanks to the GI Bill, I was able to further my studies in pathology and obtain a position as an instructor at Tufts University Medical/Dental School in Boston, Massachusetts.

At that time, the world—still only grudgingly accepting the teachings of Sigmund Freud, Carl Jung, and the rest—now quite suddenly was faced with a further extension: accept the effect of the mind on physical bodily structures and function. H. (Helen) Flanders Dunbar published her book on psychosomatic medicine and, in 1942, founded the American Psychosomatic Society. Vivian, as stated, had been a psychology major, and through her, I had gained an interest in the subject and saw possible additional relationships in this newly opened field. I conducted the first-ever experiment that established a relation between psychological directed stress and destruction of the hardest structure in the human body, the enamel covering the individual teeth. The determined results between the two entities were at a highly statically significant level of confidence, and the results were published in *Science* in 1949. They resulted in quite widespread publicity, largely in Sunday supplements throughout much of the country. Unfortunately, there was a considerable amount of disbelief by a totally reactionary dental profession and a threat to my budding career from the college's dean. Still struggling with the Freud revelations was enough. Now, he and other reactionaries were expected to advance another step. Inconceivable! Fortunately, while I was a student at the University of Rochester, my psychology professor had been Leonard Carmichael, who now served as president of Tufts. He suggested to my dean that it would be wise to accept the results of a well-designed innovative study that had provided significant results. So I was able to continue my career without interruption. Dr. Carmichael later moved on to become the head of the Smithsonian in Washing, DC.

Korea happened, and I was recalled to active duty. Since this was the second interruption in my "career," I signed over to become an officer in the regular navy, as they indicated that I would be qualified for promotion to lieutenant commander. I was sent to Camp Lejeune for marine upgrade combat training—our Geneva Conventions cards were inspected—then we were told to discard them and select our weapons "because the 'gooks' didn't give a damn" (parenthetically, another example of the generational differences in attitudes of racism and other sensitivities). My selection was the GI issue Ka-Bar knife (I still have it in my possession against regulations, I know, but am not alone), a .45, and a Thompson that still had the round magazine. (An aside: while at Lejeune, briefly assigned to a tank, I couldn't understand the communications, and being a very bumpy ride, I grabbed what was in front of me, handles with the trigger mechanism for a couple of machine guns which sprayed the field. Obviously, I was severely reprimanded.)

Next, I was assigned to Pearl Harbor, where I was head of alcohol and narcotics for FMF/Pac, with trips in and out of Korea. (*Vivian found another guy in Hawaii, and the marriage ended amicably but definitely.*) As a member of the Regular United States Navy, my assignment with the marines ended. I was reassigned to Pensacola Naval Air Station. Ashton Graybiel, a prominent physician who had been brought in to oversee the medical part of the space program where the little monkeys had been sent into space, still retained his position and was commander of the scientific activities of the base. (*One of the little monkeys sent into space—I think I recall that it was "Miss Sam"—was still alive and living there. Cute little one*). My duties at the psychology laboratory allowed me to continue my psychosomatic research but more importantly for the country (and taxpayers) was to attempt to devise a test that would eliminate DORs.

DOR stands for "drop out at own request," a release program that allows student pilots who have progressed in their training to leave if dissatisfied for any reason. One excellent student with nearly completed training left because "he just didn't feel like a marine anymore." Regardless, the program was costing the government and taxpayers hundreds of thousands of dollars. Bush Jones, a fellow member of the psychological laboratory, was a highly intelligent and innovative man with whom I was working on my own projects, and he came up with the idea that the reason for this quirk was in these individuals' personality structure. So we combined and began to devise a test that would delineate these "different" personalities. Within a couple of months, we had achieved a workable tool and began testing it with various populations. One of the more unpleasant test sites was with the prisoners in Portsmouth Naval Prison. For anyone not familiar with the facility, it is positioned in an area that seems to have nothing but dull gray skies, rain, abundant fog, and otherwise depressing ambience for extended periods of time. We actually lived in prison for two weeks to lose as little time as possible to complete studies on the population. The tenants were surprisingly agreeable and helpful, including one that gave us cause for concern before the first session. He was a six-foot-five-or-six-inch, 345-pound guy who was serving life for killing two men with his bare hands. He proved to be a pleasant, cheerful, and most cooperative individual.

Within the next few weeks, we were able to wrap it up; the test was administered to all incoming student pilots and was successful in distinguishing which would drop out early. I do not know if it still is in use, has been replaced, or whatever. However, it did save us taxpayers a lot of money for several years. The story had an interesting, perhaps somewhat irrelevant, side reaction several years later. Results of navy research routinely are published. As such, Egypt's ruler Anwar Sadat read the report. Seemingly, the dropout problem was not experienced by the US alone. I was invited to Cairo for a hands-on explanation and demonstration. It was a fascinating trip at the time.

While living in Pensacola and Vivian more or less out-of-the-picture, I met Beverly Schecter, widow of a naval officer who had been killed in action, and her young son Don. The relationship gelled nicely, and Don was a wonderful young person with whom I bonded. We were married, spent our first weekend of many in New Orleans doing all of the fun things, meeting the fabulous personalities, socializing with the local celebrities, some of whose reputations also extended far beyond—Trummy Young, Wilbur Shaw, "Satchmo" Armstrong, and more. I also was able to bring Don aboard a ship upon occasion. He and I also were great buddies and built from scratch two canoes, one of which we actually transported north when I left the service.

A pleasant side activity while in Pensacola was duck gunning on Santa Rosa Island. Offshore from Pensacola lies Pensacola Bay with Santa Rosa Island, the barrier between the bay and the open sea. It was a fabulous area for such activity, plus also helping to lower the burgeoning population of vicious feral cats. We signed out a small boat and motor from the pool to get to and from the island. Most trips were enjoyable and very productive. Unfortunately two led to some unpleasant difficulties. One began late in the afternoon and with the threat of bad weather should not have been made. However, we took off, landed, shot our limit of birds, and headed home at dusk just as the threatening skies opened up. Still no problem, except the outboard motor began to dysfunction, actually stopping completely several times. Attempting to restart a contrary outboard in heavily tossing seas during a violent downpour of rain and still keeping the boat from swamping and/or being washed out to open sea is not usually a person's idea of a fun time. Beverly had been scheduled to pick us up upon our return. The situation persisted; we already were more than an hour and a half late, so she turned on the car lights toward the direction from which we should have been returning. The lights were a welcome beacon toward the correct direction when repeatedly tossed well off course. Fortunately the episode ended with all soaking wet and miserable but at least not in the embarrassing position of explaining to the captain of a rescuing vessel what we were doing floating in the ocean.

The second unfortunate incident arising from duck gunning was a trip to the island with two of my corpsmen. A basic rule of the regular navy is that officers are not to fraternize with enlisted personnel. Completely aware of this fact but still harboring a bit of the mental attitude of reservists, I had decided these pleasant young men who were most helpful to me in working conditions deserved an opportunity to participate in an enjoyable trip. The hunt went well; no problems were encountered, and it was forgotten until two weeks later. I was called to serve on a court-martial of one of the young corpsmen. I answered the call with a negative. My immediately superior officer called me personally and asked my reason. I answered that I knew the young man well and could not in all conscious serve on such an occasion. He quickly informed me that I knew the rules, gave me a lecture, and stated that *I would* serve. He hung up immediately. He was correct; I had been wrong and should serve as directed. Demonstrating amazingly and quite stupidly naive reaction, I called the base commander and explained the situation. His answer confirmed the decision. I followed with another ridiculous, "Yes, sir, and thank you for reminding me that the service confers the title of officer but occasionally forgets the second part of the title—officer and gentleman." Obviously, my service in the regular armed forces of the United States was finished as a career, a situation that provided a large amount of relief because I gradually had discovered the rigidity of life required was not compatible with my irreplaceable civilian attitude. So also recalling an earlier incident where I had "skipped" an invitation to an admiral's formal evening to go to a luau with a bunch of Hawaiian friends on the other side of the island and the amount of negative feedback I received, I called an admiral in Washington, DC, I had known for several years and told him the story. He agreed that I was finished, so my term of duty with the United States Navy began July 20, 1950, and my resignation was accepted and went into effect February 2, 1955.

Fortuitously, a position opened for professor and chair of general and oral pathology at Washington University, St. Louis, Missouri, and we moved to a close-by suburb of the university. Here, I engaged in providing instruction in general and oral pathology and was able to enroll in a master of arts degree program in clinical psychology. I used the material I had begun while at Pensacola on my first book on the matter of psychosomatics as my thesis. I obtained the degree and expanded the thesis to become *Introductory Psychosomatic Dentistry*, which was the first describing the relationship between a dental disorder and emotionally derived tension. Appleton Century Crofts published the book in 1956 and was the first of its kind, similar to that of Flanders Dunbar for medicine.

An amusing incident during my tenure at Washington was during a visit to the closely situated Chase Hotel, which offered a well-known upscale dining room featuring prominent entertainers. We invited the dean, a PhD anatomist incidentally, and his most staid and proper wife to join us at dinner one evening when Nat "King" Cole was the main attraction. The dinner was excellent and the entertainment as thoroughly enjoyable as expected, and all was proceeding admirably until we entered the lobby. Suddenly, a loud voice called out, "John Manhold, how the hell are you?" The voice belonged to a large individual approaching rapidly with a huge smile. Upon his arrival, the conversation continued at a higher than necessary level, with continued verbalization not usually employed in general conversation. The individual was Armand Tanny, brother of Vic Tanny, who became one of the now legendary initiators of the private gyms. Armand was in the club because this evening had been Nat Cole's final night, and he was "one of the 'muscle men' in the next night's opening performance of Mae West," the quite-risqué performer highly popular at the time. I had not seen Armand since Hawaii, where he was wrestling professionally, and this had been the first time since we had grown up in Rochester, New York. During my early days, I had been quite athletic and "fun-wrestled" with both on various occasions and spent considerable time together on the beach at Lake Ontario. We lost contact and obviously went in quite different directions, with Armand attaining a most prominent position and at least twice the winner of national bodybuilding titles. So the evening was "different," and I believe secretly enjoyed immensely by the dean who was made completely aware of his wife's rigidity and discomfort.

Following such an evening's unexpected activities, it probably was quite fortunate that another serendipitous move opened. I was offered the opportunity to aid in building an entirely new school. I accepted and became chair of the Department of General and Oral Pathology for Seton Hall College of Medicine and Dentistry, Director of Research and Attending Pathologist at the Jersey City Medical Center, New Jersey.

CHAPTER 3
Serendipity Begins in Earnest

From this point, attempting to proceed in the chronological order we have been able to provide to here has come to a screeching halt. Once again, the movement to New Jersey and the newly forming school offered an opportunity to examine the vast number of openings that the 1900s offered. For individuals such as myself, a deluge of more or less simultaneously occurring and often overriding, events and/or activities were presented.

The school had been the dream of Monsignor McNulty, who was able to convince the archbishop of Newark of the need for such a move. The archbishop conferred with the Jersey City authorities, and the new school was begun in the Jersey City Medical Center, a controversial move debated for several years with respect to the necessity of separating church and state. Jersey City long had been recognized as a town where politics continued 24-7, resulting in Harold Jaegers (incidentally, "Physician of the Year") representing the medical college, and I spent one day every month in court representing our side of the controversy in often unpleasant sessions.

The development, outfitting, and staffing were accomplished by Father (later Monsignor) Michael Fronzak in accord with the results of conferences with the deans for the schools of medicine and dentistry. His expertise had been developed previously in similar positions, and he again proceeded quite frugally. Pinkney Harmon was hired as head of anatomy, and Charles Berry, a prominent professor in the department. David Opdyke was hired as head of physiology, with additional departmental personnel added as slowly as possible. To save money, I was enlisted to aid instruction in microscopic anatomy, logical because it is basic to pathology, but I was to simultaneously develop the basics of the pathology department as well as my own specified area. After all, in Mike's mind, there was no sense in wasting the money to hire a head of pathology for the medical school when it was not to be taught until the following year, and I was perfectly qualified to accomplish the job.

An amusing incident in my hiring was when Mike had come to St. Louis to interview me. After conversing for a period of time, he stopped suddenly and said, "You're not Catholic, are you?" I laughed and said I was not but couldn't understand what that had to do with teaching pathology and wouldn't hold his religion against him and assumed he intended to reciprocate. He also laughed, and shortly thereafter, perhaps startlingly for members of later generations, we shook hands, and I was hired. (For these uninitiated in the moral codes of earlier generations, a complete contract containing all pertinent facts was signed, sealed, and delivered a short time later.)

Gradually, the school project began taking shape, and instruction was initiated. Then as time progressed, even greater expansion began in my activities extending beyond chair of general and oral pathology. Added were diagnosis along with director of research and laboratories, this latter providing opportunity to establish relationships with the sizeable number of pharmacological industries in New Jersey.

One study in particular was particularly fruitful in this manner. Johnson & Johnson wanted to do a wrap-up study quickly on their newly developing product Micrin oral antiseptic. All results to date had indicated that the product was useful, but they needed the results of a "wrap-up" for their presentation to the FDA. I was able to establish space to equip and staff an entire laboratory (at their expense) to evaluate whether the product was as helpful as other studies had shown. When completed, all equipment remained for my future use. Fortunately, the results were positive, and I was able to publish quite quickly by an editor of long acquaintance in an accredited investigative journal. J & J were able to provide all necessary documentation to FDA headquarters in Maryland, and I was a member of the presenting group. The product was marketed, and the incident was particularly beneficial to my career in that it opened the way to other associations, positions, and relationships with this and other similar authoritative bodies that will be mentioned later.

I arrived home tired in midafternoon from a trip to Bethesda conferring with FDA members but stopped by my office to see if I had missed anything important. My secretary approached immediately, telling me how fortunate it was that I had returned. There was an important administration meeting that I must attend. I reported and discovered that this meeting was of gravest importance because "decisions were being made as to how much space should be designated for automobile parking space." In a most ungracious manner, I stated I couldn't care less after just finishing butting heads with some of the top mentalities in the country. I was tired, hungry, and thirsty, so I hoped they would understand if I excused myself from the intellectual morass and left. Fortunately, the assembled group knew me well, so the matter quietly disappeared. Much of the parking space agreed upon was enclosed by an easily accessible chain-link fence. One evening, when readying to go home, I found both sides of my Mercedes scored with a can opener or other sharp instrument. Repair cost was considerable, so we bought a Datsun Truck that we used for a couple of years which elicited an amusing experience.

We had driven to New York for an evening of formal entertainment, leaving the truck with an attendant. At the end of the evening, we returned and gave our parking ticket to a different attendant. He returned with the truck, looked at us in formal attire, and immediately began apologizing for getting the wrong vehicle. Of course, we quickly were able to explain that there had been no error.

Racial differences initially and for some time were a problem for the new school. We constantly found "Whitey, go home" and similar notes stuck to windshields and workers hired frequently were difficult. My personal relationships, except for the early car occurrence, were good because race had never been an issue in Rochester in those years. There actually were few black residents in the city, and one of them, Eddie Anderson, also a premed student at the university, was quite a close friend. My hires at the new school reflected my attitude. I hired the first black technician along with two Philippine technicians and the first faculty member, Ted Bolden, who had a dental degree and a PhD. Later, I hired a member of the Jewish faith, a Puerto Rican, and an Iranian ex-patriot—all at the assistant professor level.

The one potentially difficult racial incident encountered was when I had failed a black student in pathology who happened to be a Newark resident. The city at the time was populated by individuals who, for the most part, were quite educationally disadvantaged, so the student was a "unique case." A locally important and highly respected member of the city was a prominent physician who provided most of the abortions in the city. He received word of the student's failure with some indication of bias and sent me a note, saying that the man should be passed. I replied I could understand the concerns but that the student had failed quite badly, not only on a single examination but on his entire course. However, if he should prevail upon the dean and the university president that such an exception should be made, I would be most happy to comply. But I cautioned him that, as a practicing physician, he knew of the importance of understanding what he was doing to aid his patients, so he might want to think about the consequences because in all probability, if the student were to graduate, he would be practicing on his—the physician's— friends and neighbors. I received no further communication about the matter, and my relationship with the community continued quite pleasantly.

So in conclusion from the few incidents I've set forth, it is hoped that the obviousness of my opening statement is apparent. If not, the ensuing chapters should make my remarks abundantly clear. Any attempt to proceed in the chronological order we have been able to provide to this point is impossible. The basic components of all activities once initiated have remained active to varying degrees through the years and added to as other projects were found, nurtured, and grew. My love of shooting sports, established as a preteen, ballooned close to semiretirement into highly active national and international competitions; my inquisitive interests developed in early years with the publication of peer-reviewed research papers expanded and led to the publication of more texts—and later, novels— and remain foremost in my activities to this day; sculpture, acquired somewhat later, remained an interest, for which I still received a museum commission and delivered when I was in my nineties; etc.

Thus, it is our belief that continuing by category rather than chronology will provide a more meaningful approach. We already have covered the small part played by wartime activities. Accomplishments in education, scientific endeavors, book authoring, boating, national and international sports participation, extensive travel for "fun" as well as resultant of work activities, and "toys" collected along the way will follow.

CHAPTER 4
Teaching

Logically, the first to be addressed is the initial function for which I was hired—set up a teaching program. On the surface, it simply would be to follow those long in existence. The common belief? Why should training for people whose primary activity was simply to ensure people could chew their food with aesthetically acceptable teeth need more than the basics of pathological conditions as they affected the human body? (Recall the reaction to Harvard's recanting on the earlier dual-degree program mentioned earlier.)

Most fortunately, the monsignor's desiring to build the new school was an unusually enlightened man—in fact, considerably more knowledgeable and progressive in his thinking than most even realized. He wanted his school to demonstrate a new thrust. Thus, I was considered an addition of importance to his faculty and allowed free rein with the pathology syllabus and later with that of oral diagnosis.

And here it is necessary to explain to readers not familiar with the revolution that has been occurring in health care and the huge changes taking place—specifically, comprehension of the interrelationship of *all* of the parts of the human body. Regrettably, an understanding still beyond the comprehension of many, or perhaps simply a desire to remain intransigent and refuse to acknowledge "the world-shaking changes" that required rethinking. As pointed out in the preceding chapters, many in the profession still were struggling with the concepts presented by Sigmund Freud, Carl Jung, and the rest when Flanders Dunbar and the psychosomatic aspects of disease were thrust upon them. And worse from their point of view, my research was calling for even further acceptance of a mind-boggling acceptance of the relationship that included dentistry.

In accord with the new concepts, my instruction advocated routine inclusion of taking a patient's blood pressure. Such a simple procedure frequently can pick up an otherwise unknown and unexpected case of hypertension, often referred to as "the silent killer" because an individual seldom is aware of its presence before its discovery on a visit to a physician's office for other symptoms. Ordering a blood test and having the ability to interpret it, as well as ordering and understanding a complete physical upon occasion, similarly could provide early aid for the patient's health.

Another most regrettable omission even within the dentist's mind is the need to recognize and understand the far-reaching effects of dental anomalies on other parts of the body and its function. All are aware of the relevance of breathing difficulties or temporomandibular joint (TMJ) problems and are aware that they are curable with proper treatment, yet they frequently are unaware of a patient's interference with sleep situation. Why? Largely because it is not mentioned. A simple question to him/her could divulge the condition that very frequently results from correctable dental problems. In like manner, pain in the back, even in one's feet, may result from or be interrelated with oral developmental problems, and even the reverse can be true. All easily might be solved by techniques that have been devised to perform orthopedic/orthodontic therapy through nonsurgical means that will eliminate and/or repair distortions of the skull that have arisen from functional problems and/or breathing difficulties that are developing or have developed. With passing time, the growing number of investigative efforts have produced phenomenal results. And of course, the most important initiating step is to perform a complete examination and evaluation of the patient. With these results in hand and with proper knowledge of the interrelationship, palliative and even corrective measures may be taken, more frequently than not, by nonsurgical procedures that completely eliminate the problem. A sizeable number of practices have been developed throughout the country espousing this interdisciplinary approach, about which interested readers may read more if desired, starting perhaps with a relatively recent publication that further explains much of the material presented here: *Breathe, Sleep, Live, Smile* (ISBN: 9781599329208, Advantage Media Group, copyright and written by *Dr. Lynn Lipskis and Dr. Edmund Lipskis.*)

The new Seton Hall College of Medicine and Dentistry opened, our initial class arrived, and instruction was begun in a relatively orderly fashion. I had the opportunity of getting to know the class members more personally than usual in that I had just taught them histology. One in particular, Anthony R. Volpe, who was late in arriving as a result of late release from the army where he had served as an MP. Tony was a most unusual individual who became interested in the research aspects of what we were doing and provided many insights and suggested numerous innovations. Upon graduating, he joined the department, and we conducted several joint projects, one of which is a measurement still employed as most accurate within the field. Colgate, for whom I did occasional research projects, became interested in Tony. He left my department to work for them and quite quickly rose to the position of vice president for research and development. He then proceeded to advance to be one of the most prominent men in the field of dental products, research, and education—so important that he retained the position ten years past the usual time of retirement for members of industry in such a position of importance. We have continued to correspond until receipt of the immensely saddening news of his demise in October of 2020.

Of course, we had our share of problem students as the time of increased individuality arose in the sixties and students decided to demonstrate their independence. One class was quite vociferous in this area. First, they were insistent that I supply them with a more complete outline of the material I was to cover for each two-hour lecture. I explained that it had been demonstrated that students would retain more of a lecture if they personally took notes because it necessitated concentration on what was being said. The students began performing poorly on examinations during the latter part of the course, and when I informed them that as a class they were not doing particularly well, the group's leader informed me that they were learning sufficient material and that I was covering far more than was necessary, for they were "only going to practice dentistry. After all, I couldn't fail the entire class." I explained to the dean what was happening, and when it did happen, he agreed that I should offer them the opportunity of retaking the final exam, and the sizeable number who had failed either could comply or leave the school. They complied, two still failed and were removed from the rolls of the class, and all others passed with quite respectable marks. No more similar incidents occurred.

Another serendipitous occurrence. I was prevailed upon to act as associate dean for a time during which I initiated sending various professional staff members to other parts of the country and world to teach some of the progressive methods we were providing in our program. One particularly well received was in Japan, which garnered a most unexpected letter signed by Asara Mihara, member of the house of representatives and former minister of state of Japan. The letter, oversized and mounted as a plaque, presented side by side letters of commendations in Japanese and English as a thank you for sending Dr. Robert Schwartz over to provide his innovative technique.

Eventually, however, I was able to return to my department, and my research continued to extend immeasurably with the addition of more sophisticated psychological tests, electron and scanning electron microscopy, and other newly devised instruments. Results were reported to attendees in national and international conferences, then submitted to and published in peer-reviewed medical, dental, psychological, and even a couple in notable physiology journals. Further, they were incorporated in lectures to the classes as well as to various scientific organizations on invitation. Their conferences ranged throughout the country and various parts of the world. One presented in Copenhagen was particularly enjoyable when I had discovered that a new product of International Pharmaceutical Corporation was particularly helpful in providing oxygenation to healing gingival (gum) tissue. The company's president heard of the results and picked up the tab for Kit, myself, and my electron microscopic associate for the entire trip where I was reporting the results. This was not unusual but was extremely pleasant because Copenhagen is a really "fun" city. These latter activities, in turn, interrelated with a number of associated activities, some arising from the subject itself and others stemming from and/or associated with earlier occurrences.

Momentary digression to support my contention as to why sectional rather than chronologic reporting of my activities is best. An invitation to confer on wound healing at the Academy of Sciences in Moscow (to be discussed later with scientific/investigative activity) occurred not too distant from one to the Tata Institute of Fundamental Research in Bombay (now Mumbai). Associate director Fali Mehta had requested a grant from NIH to study a prominent cause of cancer in the Indian population. In the preceding chapter, we described a meeting with NIH and other representatives in Bethesda while defending a report for Johnson & Johnson and explained how this activity had other consequences as well. One was my appointment to a board examining whether organizations requesting grant funds were adequately programed to receive funding. The trip was made, inspection went well, and the grant was received.

Only tangentially pertinent, Fali had been a graduate student of mine at Tufts. He was a pleasant person, married to the daughter of a British military officer. We were entertained by him and his wife in their lovely home on Cumballa Hill, overlooking the sea with its attendant "Queen's String of Pearls" (a ring of lights lining the port area). Guests included an ambassador and his wife, another former graduate student of Tufts, and assorted other prominent local residents. The dining room was beautifully appointed with Indian boys operating large overhead paddle fans that obviously were part of the decor because the room was air conditioned. All in all, a most pleasant and charming evening until it was suggested that we have coffee and cognac on the terrace since it was such a lovely evening. Unfortunately, I have a quite sensitive sense of smell. I was able to deal with the odor rising from the ground the floor below, but it was unpleasant. After another trip a couple of years later, I have not returned to that country, so I may or may not be speaking of something still prevalent. However, at the time, cows were sacred; they roamed the streets of Bombay with no attention to their activity. Streets were filthy by our standards, and one did not go for an evening stroll without being accosted constantly by arms reaching up from the ground with, "Alms for the poor."

But now, let us turn to provide some explanation of the scientific activities in which we engaged.

CHAPTER 5
Investigative Activities

As explained in chapter 2, my first really serious investigative step was in 1949 into the newly founded area of psychosomatic medicine and employed the crudest of tools. All that existed at the time was a visual count of the evidence of destruction of tooth enamel and a pencil-and-paper list of questions that was purported to measure psychological tension. By the time I was able again to indulge in investigative activity in the area, much had changed. New and improved psychological tests had multiplied, and instruments available to measure physiological change had grown with additions such as microrespirometry and the emergence of electron and scanning electron microscopes. Before proceeding down the psychophysiological pathway, however, grant money dictated a short detour that actually provided another tool for the psychophysiological investigations. Hyperbaric pressure had become the latest trend in aides to healing; pharmaceutical houses began seeing the lucrative possibilities provided by the often stubbornly ineffective treatment of gingival (gum) tissue problems. Taking advantage of this trend, I became heavily involved in use of the Warburg method of measuring oxygen consumption by tissue, coauthoring several papers. Because of the large quantity of tissue required for the experiments, I next became interested in the Stern-Kirk microrespirometer, which could provide a QO2 (oxygen quotient expressing the quantity of that element utilized) reading from less than one milligram of wet weight tissue. The New York Academy of Dentistry was kind enough to support my early investigative work. Eventually, we were able to differentiate significant differences among normal, mildly, and heavily affected tissue, as well as gain increased knowledge of the intricacies of the difficult to use instruments. Addition of advanced psychologic testing procedures enabled demonstration of how much mentally generated tension affected the progress of wound healing. The early studies initiated use gingival tissue and eventually extended to include healing in joints and other bodily tissues that could further be accessed with electron microscopic visibility. Verification of the originally proposed Manhold hypothesis of including basic dental/oral dysfunction in the list of other psychosomatic diseases was attained when other investigators began duplicating and/or producing similar results. It took time, but one of the earlier studies was performed notably by Giddon et al.—longitudinal studies on patients with recurrent attacks of gingivitis during remission. They reported that these subjects' psychophysiologic responses to standardized stress procedures was associated with a peripheral vasomotor defect that could be reflected in elevated gingival temperatures and general hypertonicity of the digital system. If such a peripheral relationship can exist, it must extend to the gingival tissue (Giddon et al., Presentation, IADR, March 1962).

Interesting and sometimes amusing results of our studies were numerous. Perhaps unfortunately, we did not follow one lead. We had discovered a remarkable apparent difference in normal level of tissue oxygenation between different races. Assuming that a greater ability for oxygenation would prove helpful in producing better athletic prowess, such differences could indicate that one or another was superior in activities of this nature. We discovered early indications of such a relationship.

As time progressed as we moved further into general (other than oral) tissue studies, we were attempting to gather enough data to establish normal levels, pursued in part with electron microscopes.

Because my interests were in healing, they were centered on the red blood cells (O2 carriers) and their ability to be helpful. I seemed to be alone in this phase and gained the interest of Russian scientists who were the only ones studying white (infection fighting) blood cells. Moscow's Academy of Sciences issued an invitation, and Kit and I enjoyed a most interesting trip to Moscow with a week of fascinating attendant activities beyond the scientific discussions. To best summarize the trip and assorted associated features, perhaps we may again best put them in perspective by presenting material from review of a book I had been asked to do by a man who expressed his impressions of Russia in 2020. The review was posted on Amazon as well as my web page and describes M. G. Crisci's seven-day trip.

The book set forth descriptions of enlightening and frequently amusing activities from each succeeding day. Additionally a photographer of note, the author was able to provide photographs of many of the places and people visited providing an eye-opening account of Russia and its inhabitants that will surprise many, if not most of today's Americans. In my discussion, I was able to compare his experience with those I had encountered in trips to the USSR. Specifically, the author presented an appealing picture of present-day Russia that strengthened his beliefs that the alcoholism, surveillance, and otherwise general effects of seeming constant surveillance among the residents now exist only within the beliefs of the average American. Regrettably and most apologetically, I explained that some measure of reservation made it difficult to accept the author's conclusion. Granted, his trip was made during one of Putin's inaugurations following a first journey that had preceded it by two years. The freedom he noticed, and to a large extent quite ably demonstrated, today's Russia appears to be one far removed from that which long existed. To agree in part, my travels to Russia experienced some similarities to those set forth by the author but under other circumstances (i.e., not visiting as a tourist, but as a scientist visiting other scientists). We encountered most comfortable accommodations, transportation, excellent food, and entertainment and really had no sense of being under any manner of surveillance other than tight restriction with respect to picture taking. (Granted our first trip was made when Gorbachev was struggling to bring the country together following the Troika disasters.) A week after my discussions we visited St. Petersburg to see the magnificent Hermitage and had the fascinating added pleasure of attending a performance of Boris Godunov in the city's gemlike opera house. Upon boarding our plane to leave Russia, a seemingly inconsequential remark by an in-tourist representative provided a definite impression that surveillance of our activities actually had been quite extensive. Activities encountered on a subsequent trip a few years later still did not offer any definitive contrary answer; thus, two other thoughts. Within the last two to three years, I had received translations of books by Russian authors to review. None of these offer any clarification of the situation but in fact strengthens an original observation of a seeming dichotomy in the manner in which different classes or grades of citizens are observed/treated according to their main source of employment and/or activities; the other, a tendency toward observation/treatment according to religion, especially the apparent persistence of a degree of anti-Semitism, a feature one author commented on as having been accurately mentioned in my review of his book. Additionally, as continually discussed "ad nauseam" by the media, we still have the involved Russian-American political situation.

The other possibly unrecognized component in the seemingly benign assessment of Russian citizens' complete freedom: the unbidden thought that this book's author, as a well-known lecturer and as friend of the director of the Russian Cultural Center in Washington, DC., may have received some measure of unrequested and unrecognized aid in his reception and activities in Russia. But then again, and most apologetically, I am an American who had WWII memories and acquaintances as well as memories of the Cold War, Cuban fiasco, of the recurring political charges and the rest, as well as a couple of personal visits to Russia as a scientist conferring with scientists. Albeit my trips were a few years previous to Mr. Crisci's and the memories may well be influenced by the troubled times not experienced by the author of this book. Should both countries perhaps pay a little more attention to China?

But to conclude, the picture the author has provided hopefully is the correct one as he has described it and his book is highly recommended as a most enlightening and interesting read for *all* Americans to further assess and better interpret the barrage of news to which they constantly are subjected. Also, I believe little more need be said. Russia is a fascinating country with citizens who don't always agree with their ruling body but believe more thoroughly in their interpersonal relationships and that their inherent brotherhood is what keeps them together as a country. Could a small part of such thinking possibly help what was once the *United* States, or have we gone too far in accepting greed and personal desires at the expense of a country long believed to be the finest place to live and seemingly the mecca for every downtrodden individual from other countries?

But enough diversion. Passing time provided a growing accumulation of innovative investigative results to be reported. I was widely diversified and totally undisciplined in the extent of my investigative curiosity into the huge number of possibilities available. Within the next few years, in addition to the psychological aspects of disease, my endeavors led to studies of such subjects as "Glycogen content and 'basement membrane' in benign and malignant oral lesions," "Finding/reporting unusual tumors in the oral cavity" (all published in various issues of Oral Surgery, Med. and, Path. [OS, OM, OP] 1968), "Gingival Tissue

Health with Hand and Power Brushing: A retrospective with Corroborative Studies" (*Journal of Periodontology*, 1967), "A New Intra-oral Bandage" (*Journal of Oral Medicine*, 1968), "Predictive Value for Four-year Performance of Individual Parts of the Dental Aptitude Test" and "Comparison of interests, needs and selected Personality Factors of Dental and Medical Students" (*Journal of Dental Education*, 1963 and 1967), "Differential Diagnosis of Temporomandibular Area Pain" (*Psychosomatics*, 1971), and more.

In 1958, I was introduced to a particularly interesting subject: the first electric toothbrush. I received a call from Ralph Heiser, director of research and development (R & D) for E. R. Squibb, one day, asking if I could devise some tests for an electric toothbrush. After the expected discussion about people being too lazy to brush their teeth in the usual manner, I set about studying the new product designed, developed, and manufactured in Europe by Philippe E. Woog. The results of several preliminary studies were sufficient to cause Squibb to enter a contract engagement with Philippe, and in 1965, I published "Effect of the Electric Toothbrush on Human Gingiva: Histologic and Microscopic Evaluation." This provided a definitive report to satisfy the Council of Dental Therapeutics of the ADA and simultaneously to established a friendly as well as working relationship with Philippe Woog that has lasted many years.

The variety of subjects in which I gradually developed an interest obviously stimulated more requests for personally provided details of the subjects we had and were investigating. The university was pleased to have me make the trips with regard to the instructional and investigative results because it brought prestige more quickly to the newly developed educational facility. Regrettably, on a personal level the increased travel brought a considerable number of unexpected difficulties. Beverly was the daughter of an interesting woman and a man about whom I actually heard little other than basics. When I met her, she was secretary to the editor of the local Pensacola newspaper and had become an ordained minister. Her husband had been a very wealthy man with several doctorate degrees and homes in several countries. By the time I met the family, he had lost most of his money and homes, and he had an office in the business area of Pensacola, but I never knew what he did there. They were living in a small but nicely appointed home in the town along with her widowed mother, who was an interesting person in her own right. Inez was the daughter of a man from a lesser-ranking titled British family, who was too far down in the inheritance chain to receive much and came to the US where he was an itinerant schoolteacher. He married a Blackfoot Indian chief's daughter, and Inez was born. Her life was a fascinating tale of the times as she later made the trip on the Oregon Trail, lost her husband in a gunfight in the bar he owned. She retained the business, sometime later meeting and marrying a man by the name of Howard, who was with General "Black Jack" Pershing while they chased the Mexican rebel Pancho Villa. She accompanied him, and it is where Beverly experienced an incident that most traumatically affected her subsequent life and our relationship.

Bev was very young when her mother, Dorothy, had married the new husband, and because the child would interfere with their activities with his world travelling friends, she was left with her grandfather and grandmother to be raised in these most impressionable years. After a few years, unfortunately, the presence of children became a popular item among her mother's husband's friends. They descended on the Howard household to gather the child to accompany them in their somewhat nomadic life. Since the child recognized her grandparents as parents, she refused to go with them. An ensuing action of their literally hauling her out from under a bed and taking her with them obviously resulted in psychic trauma, but the story was unknown to me until, as mentioned, it began to interfere with our life. Her resistance building against my— and assumed joint—beliefs that a couple can find more enjoyment than an individual when travelling frequently to foreign countries. Ultimately it ended in divorce and when informed by the lawyer that the divorce was final, her rather vitriolic statement: "Thank God, I don't have to make those damn trips anymore!" surprised me considerably until I recalled her early childhood experiences. Our son Don was extremely disappointed and, in an altercation occurring sometime later between the two, was told she never wanted to see him again, a harsh statement of the moment that unfortunately came to pass. He had become a quite successful race car driver racing for Volvo on the Sports Car Club of America (SCCA) circuit. With a weekend off, he went to Monterey to race a new TC for a friend and was killed when a hood pin became loose and he lost visibility on a turn.

An another interesting aside of the days with Beverly is during our earlier years Bev's stepfather had died and she went to Florida for the funeral. Before leaving, she had developed a passing interest in sculpture and had started a bust of me. While she was gone, I finished it. It looked remarkably like me. I began doing other pieces, took lessons, and developed to a position where I entered competitive exhibitions, received prizes, and eventual commissions to do individual pieces—all requiring more travel. (This also will be discussed in a later chapter.)

So my regular work continued with little to no abatement. But I now had acquired an additional part-time job as a sculptor showing initial promise. Additionally, in my spare time, I was spending considerable time on my golf game, which slowly was beginning to come around. But this too will be discussed in another later chapter. For now, however, because writing obviously is such an integral part of disseminating the results of investigative procedures, it would appear necessary to concentrate next on this area of my activities.

CHAPTER 6
Writing

I have been writing and enjoying it for so many years that it has become automatic. Having begun reading voraciously while quite young, I even dabbled with attempts to compose but with little tangible results other than the term papers requested by most college and some earlier high school courses. My choice of career required production of papers detailing research results, a perfect fit for my endeavors and love affair with the English language. As already noted, the attention received from both the science community and the general public for my first scientific paper published only five years after receiving my first graduate degree and in spite of wartime activity, and subsequent investigative activity enticed Appleton Century Crofts Publishers to take notice. One of their editors approach me with respect to a book on the subject that was published as *Introductory Psychosomatic Dentistry* in 1956. More followed in a number of different disciplines:

- In 1960, W. B. Saunders published my *Outline of Pathology* (1960) with my associate professor Ted Bolden as coauthor

- *Clinical Oral Diagnosis* with contributions by a group of faculty members, published by McGraw Hill in 1965
- *Gingival Tissue Respiration and the Oxygenating Agents*, a monograph, Library of Congress # 77-02624 published 1977 at request of and supported by the International Pharmaceutical Corporation
- *Practical Dental Management: Patients and Practice* with Cecelia Black, director of the Dental Hygiene Program, UMDNJ, by Ishiyaku Euro America, Inc. Publishers
- *Illustrated Dental Terminology: A Lexicon for the Dental Profession in Four Languages* with Michael P. Balbo, director of academic resources, UMDNJ, and seventeen contributors, published by J. B. Lippincott 1985:
- *Handbook of Pathology*, coauthor Kenneth M. Klein, associate professor and director, Sophomore Medical Student Pathology Course, Year Book Medical Publishers 1987;
- *Chapters on Psychosomatic Aspects of Healing* as a Consulting guest author in several books.
- For a considerable part of these years, I also served as a science editor for J. B. Lippincott, along with my various other activities.

Finally retiring in 1987, I became Philippe Woog's medical director for a while. His main office was in Geneva, Switzerland, with factories in France. This is the same Woog whose studies we described in the last chapter.

After retiring, I continued evaluating research results for several pharmaceutical houses until into my late '70s or early '80s when the number of requests noticeably slowed. Finally asking for the reason from an old friend still in the business, his reluctant answer was that, considering the cost involved, it generally was believed that depending upon a person, such as myself (old), they were concerned that something might occur to result in a delay or possible need to restart with a new evaluator. Obviously, I had no recourse, and while grousing about it to my wife, she blithely stated, "Why don't you just write a novel?" *El Tigre* was the result and is a story within itself that led to even further unusual adventures.

While continuing my various other activities, I finished *El Tigre* within the next few months, but before even beginning to look for a publisher, I was shooting in a competition held by the Single Action Shooting Society (SASS), a group with eighty thousand plus members throughout the US and several other countries. I was speaking with another member Andy Fink, who was the editor and owner of *Shoot Magazine*, a highly successful journal for shooters of all ages. He had begun to expand and had published two books on particular weapons that had sold well. With further discussion, we agreed upon his becoming the publisher of *El Tigre*. All progressed smoothly until there was a sudden downturn in the economy, and he was forced to cease all production of his organization. Most fortunately, he was kind enough to sign over all rights for the book to me, a gracious act but one that set me on an entirely new profession. I began receiving calls from Barnes & Noble and other bookstores, stating that they could not receive any books from Baker and Taylor, the distributor. A call to B&T elicited information that I could not ship them any of the several thousand copies I had inherited because they could deal only with a publisher or other distributor. Kit and I needed to go to the statehouse in Downtown Phoenix to establish Tiger Book Distributors after paying the necessary fees. We came home with our certificate and began functioning as part of the publishing business world. We became members of the Arizona Book Publishers Association and started learning many of the problems and possible solutions for the numerous difficulties constantly cropping up.

While attending one series of meetings, we were introduced to the first electronic book readers being tested by Amazon, B&N, and two others whose names I do not recall. Various members, Kit and I included, tried them at the time but were not particularly impressed. However, we became quite active in the Arizona Authors Association and Western Writers of America as well.

In 2009, the American College of Dentists devoted an edition of their journal to creative writing. Well aware of the fact that after so many years of scientific writing as well as serving as editor for a scientific journal I had switched to writing and publishing successful novels, they were kind enough to invite me to contribute to the issue.

Entitling the article, "Writing as a Way of Life," I explained my early interest in writing and writers and having had a secondary major in college that was Elizabethan and seventeenth-century poets. I mentioned their obvious awareness of my science writing activity and admitted that my switch to include examples of fiction again was part of my serendipitous life. Added was the fact that, after spending ten to twelve hours daily in this activity, I hated to face a decline in my scientific writing activities and became a little difficult to live with resulting in my wife's remark. Also explained was that everyone in the dental profession at least roughly understands the routine of publishing the results of scientific endeavor. Results are submitted, evaluated, and if considered contributory to the field, published. However, book publication, nonfiction or fiction, requires an entirely different scenario, unless you are approached by a publishing house representative. You are advised first to acquire an agent, a difficult task for numerous reasons. But if successful, he/she will attempt to "pitch" your manuscript to any of a number of publishers. If successful, the book will be published, usually within six months to two years. The major difference between publishing scientific fact and fiction is that when completed, scientific factual material is available to all in appropriate journals. With books, at this point, your work just begins. The book must be marketed for much of which you pay unless sufficiently recognized. You, the publisher, or a hired firm that specializes in promoting books schedules you for book signings, book readings, lectures, and if all goes well, radio and TV interviews. Depending upon the individual, another most important part of publishing can be enjoyable of distasteful. If an author is an avid reader, as are many, activity with marketers is a nuisance yet has an often little-appreciated side advantage. They love to engage an author, especially if successful, in writing reviews of the work of other authors. Many do not indulge. For me, it is most enjoyable. Once more, I have acquired something else about which I can write.

So to conclude this explanation of why I write, which admittedly resembles the familiar essay style often employed by writers of a much earlier era when presenting a subject that contained many parts, I write because it is an activity in which I can totally immerse myself. Whether it is to provide facts for teaching, to present a base upon which medications can be made/distributed, because it enables me to use my imagination to create a mental picture for readers or to analyze the effectiveness of another writer's ability to provide such a picture, I am totally intrigued. Furthermore, the activity not only is most enjoyable but provides an answer to the oft-repeated need to combat some of the debilitating effects of "advancing states of maturity." It helps to keep the brain cells at a high level of activity.

During my years in writing, editing, and the publishing of research results and books, the changes that have taken place have been as huge as are those that have taken place in our culture and the direction that elements of this new culture are attempting to move the country's government. A few short years ago, I posted an opinion on one subject.

The news recently has exploded with allegations of sexual misconduct by an increasing number of women, and a few men, against individuals in an increasing number of disciplines—politicians, film producers, actors, journalists, etc., a distasteful situation that begs for consideration of the changes that have occurred in the mores of our society.

The long-held "statement of truth" that men are from Mars and women from Venus seemingly is crumbling at a highly accelerated pace. Boundaries, although still vaguely recognizable, are changing in amazing ways. For years, there have been a few women who have sought degrees and/or training in the more usually thought of male disciplines of engineering, physics, aircraft piloting, and similar, and women who have pursued careers as auto mechanics, construction workers, and the like. There also have been some men who have been more inclined to matters of fashion design and similar endeavors more traditionally thought of as more within the feminine sphere of interest. Today, however, the demarcation between the sexes has changed markedly not only in this manner but physically as well. For years, some women enthusiasts have engaged in sports such as weight lifting and boxing, but today, their number is rapidly increasing in these areas as well as expanding into even somewhat more "viciously competitive" sports such as variations of the martial arts and cage fighting. In addition, more are requesting deployment as combat soldiers with the air force, marines, and Special Forces. The formerly unheard-of acceptance of increasing numbers of individuals who have identified as homosexuals and with transgender transformation probably has provided some further impetus, if not directly, certainly by furthering change in overall attitude.

Gathering this all together, we have a population that embraces a markedly different set of mores and projects viewpoints only vaguely, if even slightly, considered a few generations back. Thus, a perfect milieu has arisen for the rash of allegations to come forth. But what about the accusations themselves? The reasons for their appearance now and in such quantity are several, and all arise from the fact that social mores have shifted so as to remove (purportedly) any stigma attached. I say purportedly because the attendant reaction will depend almost completely on the individual's position in various sections of this highly mixed and still somewhat stratified society. Many, if not most, of the complaints appear to stem from incidents that occurred many years previously and seem to be of the he says—she says variety. No doubt, women have been affronted in the past by the "unfeeling man from Mars" but could do nothing about it. Hollywood sexual misconduct has been common knowledge for generations and aberrant behavior by persons in any position overseeing others of lower employment status similarly has been widespread until recently. Women, as well as some men, with elevation of women to higher levels of management, have been affected and have carried a resentment, and rightfully so, for years. The problem: society closed their eyes to the activity, so there was no recourse. With today's new mores, the time has arrived to gain release from this long-carried burden.

The present "rash" of explosive allegations seemingly generated against prominent political figures is a newer wrinkle, however. Because of the recent expansion in today's vitriolic and highly contradictive public view of the political situation, one cannot help but feeling that it does not seem to be as genuinely honest as the other cases mentioned. That a considerable amount of its prominence at this particular time might be as a specific result of this factor. Jack Kennedy's activity was well known but seldom mentioned, as was his successor's. Clinton's extensive and well-documented activity brought forth impeachment proceedings but no positive action. However, today, all hades is breaking loose. The allegations are rampant and may well be true. However, many allegations are from activities from many years earlier. There is absolutely no question these may well arise from actions that have caused a burden to be carried for many years that only now with the present change in mores may be brought to light and shared. But regrettably, suspicion does raise its ugly head because accusations are brought against prominent political figures only now when there had been no accusations presented through their many years of public service, even at the time when they would have been heard because similar charges were being leveled against a then president. There is no doubt about the seriousness of situations of rape or other use of force, but allegations of improper language or "touching inappropriately" do seem a little difficult to accept from women now in their middle years or slightly more. They are of the generation that more often than not would giggle when recounting "having their bottoms pinched" while in Italy, a well-recognized activity there. And *please* do *not* think I am treating this matter lightly. I just believe with so many important issues to be dealt with, this inordinate amount of time spent on whether someone inappropriately "touched" someone or "suggested an impropriety" is slightly irrelevant and that it may be more specifically politically based. It could be as a result of an individual wanting again some attention (aware of waning attractiveness, insufficient attention from spouse, or other), for compensation to provide accusation, or lack thereof (apropos the recently revealed disgusting "slush fund," unwittingly taxpayer supported) which was available to pay off congressionals accused of improper advances. *Or* it could be genuine. It is the reader's decision to be made only after impartially considering the evidence produced. Regardless, the overabundance of media attention compared to the gross *undercoverage* of important issues facing the country today also is becoming revolting. What has happened to honest journalism?

A friend who read the article provided his thoughtful comments. I believe that any more left-leaning readers who have persisted this far may be uncomfortable with his comments. But anyway...

> John, Your article makes sense on a lot of levels, especially the effort you made to cover the subject. It seems that people avoid looking at all sides of an issue to come to quick conclusions and immediate solutions. Liberalism and globalism have created a real void in discipline and eroded any foundation for making sound decisions. Issues like sexual misconduct create a lot of confusion for liberals because they have no solid moral base to begin with. They get twisted up in a knot when they are forced to deal with the issues, looking only to the polls for guidance on what to say. How silly is it to think that our leaders and lawmakers need training for sexual harassment? Do they need kindergarten 101? I worked with sexual offenders for many years and everyone in government knows the deplorable state of our society

and the human condition on this matter. It's funny to see how shocked they are when someone is caught. With a media that promotes sex and takes every opportunity to undermine our government to create a socialist state, it is not far-fetched that sexual allegations are used as a tool for political gain. Thanks for your article.

But to summarize, I am sure that any of you who have deigned to read this lengthy bit will have your own accepting or contradictory thoughts. However, I believe no one will take umbrage with my main contention: the mores of our society sure have changed and immensely so within the last few generations when compared with those originally extant in mine. For a brief comparative note, I give you the following: A man by the name of Hutchinson served on a destroyer that participated in operations that took him from Guadalcanal to the signing of Japanese surrender at Tokyo Bay. I had the privilege of reviewing his book some years ago and well remember how succinctly he put into words what most members of our generation who fought in WW II believed. Specifically, he stated:

We Hope to be remembered as the products of a different country and society from what the United States of America has become in the last fifty years. Products of a far more disciplined society with rather rigid moral and social standards to which everyone was expected to conform given how society chastened and disciplined offenders. The way of the transgressor was hard. We were taught individual responsibility, that evil is due to character flaws in the individual and not to the shortcomings of society.

Since then, we have learned that some of this strict rigidity may not be totally acceptable. That there are certainly "shades of gray." However, we *were* taught self-reliance and furnished with a basic moral code to employ when making decisions, and we *were* "one nation, under God." We survived a *real* depression without "handouts" from the government, fought a global war and did so undivided. Any reader surviving this far again will have to make up his/her own mind as to what might be best for the country.

Another feature that must be taken into consideration with the changes in our society is exemplified by another book I reviewed a few years back written by John Dennehy, titled *Illegal*.

Plot: Grossly unhappy with the political climate in the United States and particularly resenting the rising nationalism (opposed to true patriotism) with its belief in their superiority to people of other countries and obviously unable to effect change, the protagonist decided to leave the US searching. He discovered a job offer to teach English in Ecuador. He boarded a plane, entered the country, began teaching, and felt "at home." Ecuador during this period was in a near-chaotic situation with a disastrous political system (elected eleven presidents in seven years), rampant corruption and bribes required for most activity. Residents had developed a rather freewheeling attitude toward governmental authority, starting numerous road blockages and more. Completely enamored with the citizenry and of their temerity to exhibit their displeasure, he enthusiastically joined them in their frequent "revolts." He also discovered the "love of his life" in a young woman who lied to him, had occasional other sexual liaisons, and fought violently with him after their occasional drinking bouts. Still, his love persisted, and with Lucia, plus his growing attachment to other friends he had made, he was willing to illegally cross the border several times, an activity he believed "necessary." He had been deported once, and the requirement to leave and return every sixty to ninety days required to reside in Ecuador would mean exposure of this fact if legal crossing were attempted. The story continues by following his various activities within Ecuador and other countries during his extended stay and finally into the election of the popular presidential candidate who was "going to provide a government totally for the good of its citizens." Unfortunately, this latter period in residence was that in which this "good" president gradually demonstrated massively corruptive activity as well, resulting ultimately in delusion descending upon him and accompanied sadly by realization that Lucia also was no longer the "love of his life."

In my discussion, I stated that this autobiographical tale provides interesting observations on Ecuador in an unfortunate period from which it finally recovered, although again showing rumblings of political discord. Seemingly, the author also has used this as a platform to project fundamentally a political viewpoint that entreats additional commentary because that offered is most interesting as the beliefs set forth by many impressionable naive young people today, many of whom have not been deprived or abused but rather provided considerably more than life's basics. As described, he was afforded a good life with his biological family's constant support, including even continuing financial assistance when needed during this "rebel period." He quite adeptly points out several problems facing US residents but particularly centers on nationalism and border control, accusing the US of acting most unfairly in both cases. Summarily he states:

> Borders are everywhere they exist between nations…, and they exist inside each of our minds. It doesn't have to be this way…products have freedom of movement. Why shouldn't the people who made those products be afforded the same freedom?…why shouldn't admission to migrants be the norm, and their exclusion the exception?… Within the European Union, though travel is unrestricted, each nation maintains its unique identity…(also) there are a multitude of unique hubs that exist within adjacent neighborhoods.

His assessment, ideally speaking, is absolutely correct. But most regrettably, realism seems to indicate a naive failure to assess the basic components. First, "It doesn't have to be this way" completely ignores some individual issues (see below). Second, a huge difference in the numbers of individuals who wish to immigrate to various countries exists; the largest number is those wishing to immigrate to the United States. Here, they've arrived for years, proceeded through immigration procedures, remained initially within their own enclave but gradually accepted the mores of our country and moved to become participating United States citizens, accepted the laws, and enjoyed the freedom offered that in many ways far exceed that encountered in others. Parenthetically, and most unfortunately, today's immigrants cannot seem to "fend for themselves," causing a drain on the citizens for financial aid often for sustained periods. Third, individual differences. Everyone wishing to immigrate does not have the preferably altruistic attitude. Some come to "send money back home," some have criminal records, and some, like the author, might indulge in illegal activity "because it was necessity to live in the manner that was most satisfying for him," justifying the illegality as something that did no harm, and he was dealing with corrupt individuals anyway—absolutely true but still an illegal act that could have been avoided in the first place when he decided to "throw himself into the local revolts." A country must be aware of such an individual because the "next time," harm might be done. Fourth, he touts the free borders of the European Union, completely ignoring the magnitude of the resulting problems. In most, local worker/economy has suffered, but more impressively, criminal activity has greatly accelerated. The author does mention "unique hubs exist in adjacent neighborhoods" but does not include the fact that their strict adherence to their own rigid customs too frequently is distinctly incompatible with those of their new society. Perfectly acceptable, *except* that with increasing frequency, they are blatantly attempting to impose their mores upon the inhabitants of the country that has been kind enough to welcome them. Reason certainly seems to indicate that such activity definitely provides an unfortunate but undoubtedly cogent reason for existence of borders. Regrettably, these features are not taken into account in this otherwise well-written but rather critical depiction of his "home" country that seems somehow to have provided him with most of "the better thing in life."

Conclusion: I hope that anyone reading this review will not interpret it as "taking sides." It simply is commentary that would seem necessary to include when reading this seemingly highly politically motivated presentation in the form of an autobiography offered by a young man who appears only to have performed a surface examination of a multifaceted, seemingly unsolvable dilemma (and as an aside, has included, unfortunately, a number of errors pertinent to Ecuador).

I gave the book a 4 star rating as a well-written autobiography/political commentary with a note that missing details were provided here. But now, I should like to provide an additional thought: Now older and somewhat matured, the author extolls the merits of his present employer, the United Nations, and his coworkers. Interestingly, this is an organization that appears to be much like himself. The United Nations, according to a report (2010) of the Heritage Foundation Entitled "U.S. Funding of the United Nations Reaches All-Time High." They note that the US has been the largest financial supporter since the UN founding in 1945 and currently is assessed twenty-two percent of its regular budget and more than twenty-seven percent of its peacekeeping budget (associated exemplary figures: 516.3 dollars regular, 2,182 dollars peacekeeping [2011]). However, US provides additional assessed contributions to many other UN organizations plus voluntary contributions to many more. For example, the OMB lists US total contributions as more than 6.347 billion dollars in FY 2006, which is more than one billion more than for 2005, obviously indicating a budgetary rise and consequential demand for more US money. Regrettably, as so viewed on TV, it usually is accompanied by other nation's statements that "we should do more."

Doesn't this sound somewhat similar to the author's position in which he seems somehow to find this country to be thoroughly disappointing and somewhat demeaning in our attitude to other countries? An attitude that fails to recognize that it was from this country he received a privileged upbringing and from citizens of this country (his parents) financial aid every time he needed it. Amusingly, it once again brings to mind Hutchinson's book, where he pointed out that our generation had survived a devastating depression followed by a brutal war and had gained the ability to resolutely "stand on our own two feet" independent of others, and that this trait had allowed the country to rise to the position of the most powerful in the world. Are today's younger citizens missing something? And I repeat, I do not wish to be accused of "taking sides politically." I am merely attempting to supply facts not considered by the author and perhaps others (?) of today's younger generations.

Readers not particularly interested in this aspect of my career, if you haven't already departed, you might just possibly be interested in just one more thought with respect to a now historical aspect of writing that has evolved because of the rapidity of movement of the technical age in which we are living.

Several years ago, after returning to Florida, I was offered a position at the University of South Florida to teach a course in writing and publishing. At the time, selling books had become a problem of increasing importance with many "middle-income" authors finding it difficult to still be able to "make a living." I titled the article "Selling Books in Today's Chaotic Market," and it was published in both the *Arizona Authors' Monthly* and the *Florida Writers' Quarterly*. The article reads:

> I have been involved in book publishing since 1956 when Appleton-Century-Crofts published my first textbook. Some years later I served as a Science Editor for J. B. Lippincott, and six years ago I was forced into marketing and distribution of books. In those first, and for a large number of years thereafter, book publishing had a precise pattern. Publishers selected the titles, signed the authors to contracts, gave standard royalties, printed the books, and sold them to distribution companies. The distributors then resold them to wholesalers, retailers and finally stores. Discounts were established and standardized, and everybody made money.

Suddenly, Print on Demand became available, avoiding more costly traditional publishing methods, and many new publishers and authors entered the picture. The large publishers thought they could eliminate this new influx by spreading the word that these books were inferior. POD publishers unfortunately aided the spread of such thoughts by publishing anything for anybody who would pay the price.

A few POD publishers got smart. They opened distribution centers and began to be more selective in what they published. By this time the public was so brainwashed about the inferiority of self-published books that it took some time before they began to find that many are well-written, well-edited and well worth purchasing. Gradually, and fortunately, the strong negative opinion about self-published books is beginning to diminish.

The POD revolution had not even concluded before there was another technical advance—the e-book. And it is this latest that has become a compelling force wreaking havoc in today's publishing-marketing industry—witness Borders recent problem and B&N's so far futile search for a buyer.

I became acutely aware of how these matters could affect the author, and more especially the mid-list and new author, when the local university here in Sarasota, FL. provided me with an opportunity to provide a series of lectures on writing/publishing. It began when an acquaintance in marketing asked if I had read a recently published article. I had, and immediately became aware of how limited the offering was for many writers. It was typical of these articles and pitches by professional marketers. It stressed the importance of using the numerous group-contacting methods technically available today. Additionally, most of the article was directed toward the entrepreneur and the person who has written a book selling something or offering some service. The material provided little help to the fiction writer, except in a general way.

I have believed for some time that the aid provided by the group contacting methods may not be as effective as constantly claimed. With the stimulus of providing information for others, I began perusing the literature and found some most interesting results.

In one article, Michael Davis (a romance/ mystery author of some note) reported results of a study he did on selling his books over a four-month period. He rated 21 activities he used to promote them by assigning a rating from 100 points down and considered any score above 50 as effective in terms of time spent. He found that those rated below 50 were of little, to no, help. His results:

Special recognition (Author of the Year, and similar), 100 points

Reviews, 90 points

Site participation and Contests, 70 points

Shared Linking, 50 points

Then, came the rest:

Interviews, Special chats, Video Trailers, Bookmarkers, all at 35 and 30 points. Blogs gained a rating of 25 points and the rest fell even below these with Facebook, Myspace, Twitter, etc., rated at a mere 5 points.

Another interesting article I found was an interview with three New York Times Best Seller authors, Tess Gerritsen, "retired M.D. and eclectic writer," David Baldacci and John Gilstrap, about their feelings with respect to the importance of Facebook, Twitter and Blogs. Briefly, their opinions were:

Tess Gerritsen—"Certainly one more thing to worry about and they suck time from our schedules. Does it make a difference in sales? Probably some, but I don't know how significant it is."

Baldacci—"Twitter and Facebook are helpful but also one more thing to keep track of. I don't spend a lot of time on either."

Gilstrap—I participate in a group blog (killzoneauthors.blogspot.com) on Fridays ("shameless promotion gets tiresome after a while"), but I don't know how people maintain solo blogs. As for Twitter and Facebook, I have accounts in both, but I confess that I don't really get it."

All of these best-selling authors seem to be expressing an opinion that is the same as one that I have harbored for some time. These techniques that publishers, marketers, and others, are insisting to be of utmost importance as a means of selling books, may be of questionable value. Instead, they may provide merely other distractions that keep you from your more productive activities. True, some authors may indeed find these venues to be helpful. However, my thoughts of the matter—that they seem to be overrated—do not seem to be mine alone.

It is my firm belief that to be even moderately successful in today's market, you must have a sizable group of readers with whom you share a common interest. Without it, publishing and selling novels is quite simply a crap shoot. I have been able to establish such a group with activities that cover a number of years. Marketers postulate that such a group can be established through the methods they suggest. However, even they do not provide specifics to accomplish this, and in using Facebook and the rest, they constantly set forth the admonishment that "care should be taken not to appear as if you are "pushing' your book." So, again, a fine line must be negotiated for a questionable result.

My suggestion to my students is: if they don't have a sizable group with whom they have established a common bond, or if they cannot establish one, they had better really enjoy writing, because their sales may not come anywhere close to their expectations. There is an adage that has been around for many years in the writing profession: "Don't be in a hurry to give up your day job."

I have not previously expressed these, my opinions, to other than my students because they provide a very negative picture. However, I now believe that any writer who wishes to become 'a published author' must bring his/her expectations to a plausible level. My hope is that, as with my students, writers will continue to write for the pure enjoyment and sense of accomplishment that the activity brings, and accept any monetary recompense as a most pleasant and additional result.

So with this acknowledgement of the rapid ingression of technological advances into the staid old career of writing, I think it might be best to move on to the next, although concurrent, chapter in my life's endeavors.

CHAPTER 7
Sculpture

My interest in sculpture began in New Jersey while still engaged in the previously mentioned activities. Beverly's stepfather passed away, and she returned to Pensacola for the funeral. Before leaving, she had gained a passing interested in sculpture and had blocked out a bust of me. One evening, I examined her just-begun project, became interested, went to work, and finished it before she returned. It was an easily recognizable image of me and stimulated my search for a local instructor. I contacted Ward Mount, wife of a physician who lived relatively close, and had been president of a certain New Jersey Artists Society. After seeing my completed bust, she agreed to give me private lessons that could fit in with my sliding schedule. I completed several pieces with her. She suggested I attempt to exhibit them; I did and took several prizes in New Jersey shows. To expand my education, I enrolled in a sculpture course in New York in the new school and studied under Chaim Gross and Bruno Lucassi. Chaim was a carver, which, along with Ward Mount's instruction, allowed me to carve clay as well as my later endeavors with stone. Most users of clay build up their pieces by adding the substance. With carving, you simply take the number of blocks of clay you believe will suffice and meld them together with a large wooden mallet. When finished, you begin to carve out the subject you wish to make. When completed, it is taken to a foundry where a plaster cast is made, the clay is removed, and the molten bronze poured in. When completed, you apply the patina you desire, and that's it.

Wood carving is self-explanatory with the difficulty factor dependent mostly on the quality (hardness, possible fracture lines, or differences in the hardness) encountered. Hawaiian Koa wood is a pleasure to use because of its deep rich colors and the varying grain patterns. It is legendary in Hawaii, and at one time, only certain classes of natives could use it with King Kamehameha owning huge forests. When cattle were introduced to the big island, much of the Koa forests were destroyed, so today, the wood is revered, and its sale is restricted to trees that already are dead. Monkey pod wood, also known as Parota, is another exotic hardwood, although more popular for larger items such as coffee tables, which seem to generate explosive popularity. One of the largest and oldest of these trees is a national treasure in Venezuela. A monkey pod tree can grow to fifty feet or more and the top forms a huge umbrella shape. Lignum vitae, oak, and similar, on the other hand, are extremely dense and not particularly desirable selections for carving.

Stone similarly provides different grades of desirability for carving. Granite, although no doubt most durable, is not particularly pleasant to carve, whereas soapstone is delightfully easy. It is found everywhere, in multicolors, and has been used for carving for centuries. It is durable and heat resistant. African wonderstone, technically pyrophyllite, is another delightful stone to carve as is alabaster, usually a white translucent or possibly more opaque stone that may be found with slightly different tints. It is formed from fine-grained gypsum.

A couple of asides with respect to sculpture from my personal perspective, the first with respect to alabaster. I had purchased a piece of white translucent alabaster to carve a seahorse. All went well until I began on the head. I carved into a previously undetected section of opaque stone. I completed the piece but could not really offer it for sale because it did not have the translucency for which people purchased translucent alabaster. With a light mounted behind such a sculpture, the effect really is quite appealing. Unfortunately, the same thing happened a second time when the piece was depicting a representation of the Olmec era. Actually, I was able to rescue the piece because I reasoned the stone should be able to absorb water. It did, and after five hours of boiling it in water, I had a piece of opaque alabaster in which I carved a different facial expression on the reverse side, mounted the piece on a rotary base, and named it Olmec Dilemma.

The second aside has to do with sculpture done in any stone media and may present a tendency that represents a thought pattern that probably is mine and mine alone. Occasionally, I will encounter a piece of stone that "has its own idea of what it will represent." I had acquired a piece of steatite in which I had intended to carve a head of a Chinese Mandarin or person of position/influence. The stone just would not respond. Instead, it insisted on becoming the head of a ram. I made the required adjustments using a bush hammer in the proper places, carving in a ram's horn on each side, and finally had a remarkable resemblance, which I entitled Aries.

During this time, I continued sculpting when I found time. I was living on the top floor of a high-rise apartment in West New York, New Jersey, and was able to rent a basement room that I turned into a studio. The living quarters presented a magnificent view of the city of New York that was particularly spectacular at night. I began entering my pieces in numerous New York as well as the previously entered New Jersey art exhibitions. With increasing frequency, they were accepted and, surprisingly to me, soon began receiving numerous awards. The awards brought recognition. Of particular interest was the first place award received in Paris, France, for my sculpture Nude—a modern high-polished bronze that initiated some international recognition that brought commissions on this level as well as those more regularly offered within the United States (e.g., of Piccard collection in Bern, Switzerland, and one of Kikiku Yamada, wife of Toyotaro Yamada, former executive, Toyota Motors, Nagoya, Japan). Of interest within the States perhaps are *Ova*, a polished bronze in the Sloan-Kettering collection, New York City, and a dark-brown patina stevedore entitled *Days of Glory Past*, depicting such a person found on the waterfront docks in many New Jersey cities. Upon purchase, it was to reside in the mayor's office in West Orange. A second copy, incidentally, is owned by Fairleigh Dickinson University, New Jersey. (Traditionally, a vague rule exists that seven copies legitimately can be made as "originals," although Rodin was accustomed to make a couple more.)

An amusing incident occurred with respect to *Ova*. An oncologist by the name of Dr. Bernie Koven commissioned me to make a piece that could be okayed by the art committee for decorating the Sloan-Kettering Hospital in New York. I submitted a design they liked, proceeded with the clay model, and invited them to view it before casting. They arrived, Kit provided tea and crumpets, and they were quite satisfied. Mrs. Lawrence Rockefeller asked what it was called. Not really having decided upon a name, I answered with a question of what she thought it might be. She answered that it brought to mind a collection of unusual eggs. Immediately I responded. "How observant. The title is *Ova*."

With respect to actual positions held within the art community, I have quite frankly been far too actively engaged simultaneously in too many projects to take any administrative roles other than director of sculptor at Ringwood Manor, New Jersey, which sits in a small section of the state that requires a short journey through New York State to arrive. Also, I have taught sculpture to individual students occasionally through the years, but a little over a year ago, I finally stopped accepting commissions and doing any sculpture for that matter. (I was nearing the one-hundred-year mark.) My last sculpture commission was done just shortly before this. It was a bronze portrait of the founder of the Single Action Shooting Society (SASS), whose SASS name is "Judge Roy L. Bean," after the original who administered "The Only Law West of the Pecos." The bust resides in the SASS Museum in Colorado.

So to conclude, sculpture has been an engaging occupation, which I have been able to fit in among my other vocations/avocations through quite a number of years. It has been a most enjoyable pursuit that has provided many hours of pleasurable relaxation. It also has garnered national and international awards and recognition far beyond anything I could have imagined as well as bringing me into contact with numerous fascinating individuals, some of whom became friends of many years. In all, involvement in creating a tangible object that you have imagined is a truly rewarding experience.

CHAPTER 8
The Joys and Other Aspects of Owning Boats

Boating is an activity that has expanded immensely through the latter part of the 1900s and into the present. In large part, this has occurred as a result of the steady increase in income. Today, anyone can own a vehicle that propels them over the water even if it is only a paddle board or similar. Early in the twentieth century, boat ownership, maintenance, docking fees, and the rest were quite costly. Employment in the educational field is not a particularly good way to gain any semblance of wealth. Nevertheless, with gradual elevation in collegiate level teaching position coupled with other further-reaching opportunities, things can open up (e.g., guest lectures, consulting). But to begin, separately and together, Kit and I have experienced most of the idiosyncrasies of boat ownership. Kit personally owned a powerboat for waterskiing, at which she became most proficient. My boating history is a rather lengthy affair that began with sailing on my father's thirty-eight-foot gaff-rigged ketch on Lake Ontario, including numerous trips to Canadian ports. These early days were at a time in the twentieth century with which I am sure most present-day boaters will find unbelievably amusing. It was a period when one left the club dock by coming aboard dressed in coat and tie before changing into more appropriate attire. Upon returning, the ritual was reversed before leaving your vessel.

But with respect to personal ownership, Kit and I purchased our first boat while I was still employed by the university and living in New Jersey. It was a forty-two-foot sun runner built in the Northwest. It had a top speed of a little over thirty-five knots, open cockpit, and sleeping and eating quarters forward below deck. We kept it berthed at the marina in Forked River on the New Jersey Coast. The marina was close enough for us to reach in reasonable time and offered excellent and enjoyable seafood restaurants nearby in case we preferred not to cook while in port. We became members of the Lackawanna branch of the United States Power Squadron and began learning all we could about deepwater boating.

An aside here is the matter of a most rewarding accomplishment by me, who had been told by my electrical engineer father to "go become a doctor because you would never make an engineer." The division received a commendation from R/C Carl F. Scharff (marine navigation chairman) Marine Electronics Course Comm. It reads:

"CONGRATULATIONS"
MARINE ELECTRONICS

We convey our congratulations to John H. Manhold of your squadron for making a perfect score on the Marine

Electronics Examination he took recently. This is something that is attained by only a very small percentage of our students and we consider it a tribute to the effort and dedication of both the student and the instructor. Keep up the good work.

Because we began contemplating longer trips, we decided to investigate larger boats that would provide for more pleasant live-aboard accommodations and an ability to proceed at a more leisurely pace while making longer trips. We finally settled on a marine trader trawler because of its flared bow which made it a "dryer" boat than the perhaps more well-known Grand Banks, whose bow was quite narrow. We had to wait for *Ketita II* since she was made in Taiwan but were most satisfied upon its arrival. These vessels are constructed for relatively long-range cruising and have a forward stateroom with double bed and a head on the portside just at the bottom of the ladder (stairs) that descended to this area. A second bunk that could be lowered from the portside overhead was in the salon. The salon contained two tables along the portside in front of the long cushioned couch that extended along the inner wall of the cabin. This couch/bench was wide enough to also function as a lower berth. The starboard side included a sliding door for entrance to a helm that connected to another on the open canvas-protected flying bridge above. A stove and large refrigerator with a TV mounted on top along with open space completed the starboard terminating the inner cabin, which finished with double doors to the outer deck. All of the interior woodwork was elaborately and beautifully carved teak. The open stern area was relatively spacious, and we carried here a motorcycle for land transportation when required. We had mounted a motor-driven hoist (davit) topside to unload and retrieve the vehicle when required.

The ladder leading topside was on the starboard side and topside there was considerable deck space leading forward to the helm and throttles connecting with those below. A comfortable seat at the helm, removable canvas top, several deck chairs, a table, and the radar tower completed this area. The engine room was not particularly "roomy" in which to work because Kit had twin Lehman Marine Diesel Super 275 engines installed.

With respect to the motorcycle, it proved to be a really worthwhile addition because more frequently than one could imagine, it can fulfill a real need. One of these times was on one of our "shakedown" cruises in the new *Ketita II*. Upon arriving and gaining permission to dock overnight at a small yacht club that could not provide dinner, realization occurred that unfortunately we had failed to stock our larder. The attendant/dockmaster told us about a very good restaurant a few miles away and offered to get a taxi, which being in a small town "would be a little expensive" and that the eatery also was "upscale." We said we would use our motorcycle if he would provide directions. He complied, we dressed appropriately, off loaded the cycle, and took off. As we arrived at the restaurant, a couple was just leaving, noticed our vehicle and proper attire, and with a straight face asked me where Kit hid her secret tattoo? The restaurant's ambience was charming, the dinner was great, and we saved a considerable chunk of money on transportation besides avoiding going hungry because of an uncalled-for mistake.

After a few more short cruises, we finally felt familiar with the new boat (its equipment and idiosyncrasies), sold our home on Shunpike Road in Chatham Township completely furnished, gave the Mercedes 240 Diesel to a relative for two thousand, and began our journey to the condominium we had purchased completely furnished on the top floor with large windows and a sizeable balcony overlooking John's Pass and the Gulf of Mexico. In all, quite a lovely place, except for a smaller hurricane that passed through when we were unsure whether the windows and glass balcony doors would survive even though reinforced as much as possible. Our unit came with our own dock, and with a sharp turn on departing, we were able to proceed to the entryway to John's Pass that could have tricky currents upon occasion. These latter were slightly problematic on our return from a cruise. One engine had developed a problem, but Kit, in her normal completely dependable style, was able to keep it functioning adequately to allow us to get through the Pass safely.

Before moving to Florida, I had made frequent trips to visit my parents who had moved to St. Petersburg upon retiring. Thus, my knowledge of the general area was quite extensive and decided the place at John's Pass fitted our needs quite well. It was close to the Pass-a-Grille Yacht Club, which we visited several times before moving and had been offered membership. Somewhat later, we also joined St. Petersburg Yacht Club (although St. Pete acquired Pass-a-Grille a few years later).

St. Pete was one of the initiators of the Florida Council of Yacht Clubs, which joined together in reciprocity so that a member was welcome to use the facilities of any of the others for overnight docking accommodations with member's charges referred to his/her own club. St. Pete, incidentally, is particularly well-known in that it sponsors several national/international sailing regattas and also boasts a number of famed members who have scored Olympic gold, sailed in the America's Cup, and have built world renowned sail and powerboats. As members, we were offered the finest of accommodations on our many cruises to various ports of the United States as well as the Bahamas and some of the islands in the Caribbean. On a golfing trip to the UK, we even were able to enter the Royal and Ancient Golf Club as members of St. Pete when playing the old course at St. Andrews.

An amusing aside in our early days at Pass-a-Grille was when a member of a group who had boated in from Naples for the weekend could not get his boat started. He asked the commodore if there was a reliable engineer or mechanic who could help. He was informed that it would be difficult and could be expensive as they did not like Sunday morning work. But then he said, "Wait. A relatively new member of the club might be able to help." He called us, and Kit said she would be happy to help but wanted to finish breakfast first. After finishing, we got into the car and drove over to the club. She had the motor started in twenty minutes, and he was on his way. The most interesting part we only learned later. Apparently, the owner almost suffered a heart attack when a lovely young woman drives up in a yellow Rolls-Royce on a Sunday morning, gets her tools out of the trunk, and approaches, asking where the problem was. The crowning moment of course was when she did not charge him for the favor.

With respect to the Rolls, I had wandered into a show room and happened to speak with the young German proprietor who offered me a proposition—a new Rolls plus a few bucks if we returned it after driving it for one year. At that particular time, Rolls were popular in Germany, but the taxation on their purchase was extremely high unless they were at least a year old used car. It was an enjoyable as well as profitable few years before their laws changed.

But back to boating. We thoroughly enjoyed our travels and found the trips to the various islands fascinating but not infrequently a bit harrowing. In the Bahamas, many of the islands and cays you will not even find named on most maps of the region. Entering to dock may even be treacherous. I remember one of the unnamed had a large rock in the middle of the channel that was only visible at low tide; another had a very tricky channel, but they at least did offer a most welcome but naturally somewhat costly pilot service.

Some of the other less-pleasant occurrences encountered in long-range boating are generated by the weather. But then there also are such factors as "sketchy" information not infrequently provided by "locals." Buoy positions may not have been moved when required, or reports and/ or charts may not have been brought up to date for one reason or another. To provide a few details of the effects of each of these situations, we'll mention a few for your contemplation.

On one of our trips to Nassau, our radar spotted extremely heavy weather descending on the island. Coming from the open sea with nothing else available for miles around, we had no choice but to continue on into port. The weather caught up with us, and we were most fortunate to make port safely with God's help when other craft were losing much if not all of their electronics. A large sailboat lost its main mast from a lightning strike, and numerous others suffered various other disabling problems. It really was quite a white-knuckle experience. And with respect to my reference to God, please do not be disturbed by the statement. It does not entail any significant fact other than simply a specific personal belief in and respect for a higher power that has been operative many times in my life and would appear, from my readings and occasional remarks by others, would be shared by others. You will recall my quotation earlier by Hutchinson, the sailor whose wartime journey took him from Guadalcanal to Tokyo Bay during WWII. There also is an applicable phrase purported to have been coined during that war, which states, "There are no atheists in foxholes." Anyway, there is a fascinating feature of storms of this magnitude whether in local or foreign waters, although probably more uniquely visible when met in larger expanses. The water is completely smooth just before the endless sheets of rain begin to descend. Other storms of similar, slightly less, or even more violent and of hurricane strength regrettably are an unpleasant part of long-range cruising. We have been forced several times to find "hurricane holes," well-sheltered areas where usually storms can be "ridden out" with two or three anchors properly placed.

Another occasion of interest was during our trip "Around the Big Wheel" from St. Pete north through the waterway to the East Coast, up the coast in and out of the intracoastal to the Erie Canal (which was still navigable) to Lake Ontario, the rest of the Great Lakes to Sault Ste. Marie on Lake Superior, back down to Chicago, the Chicago River to the Mississippi, Kentucky Lakes, Tombigbee, the Gulf, and home. One evening, miles from any port, we found a likely spot to drop anchor at an area used to store barges not in use. For some reason, we were uncomfortable with tying up to any of the large vessels and chose an area quite removed. During the night, a sizable storm passed through, and in the morning, our discomfort with a possible vessel tie-up was found to have been justified. They were a jumbled mess. Another time, we started the completely overcast day and were hailed by a sizable sailboat, who asked where we were headed. His electronics had been knocked out during the overnight storm, and the day was completely overcast. He discovered he was not heading in the direction he thought he was going.

Our acquaintance with problematic "locals" can best be described with our return to local waters and running aground in the middle of the channel in Cedar Key on Florida's west coast. Upon radioing in, we were informed that one was required to stay a little more to port when negotiating their channel. A recent hurricane had changed the channel a bit, and they had not as yet been able to move the buoys or even placed a warning sign. Besides, "everybody knew about the change anyway" (?).

With respect to NOOA, on Lake Michigan, much of their information seems to coordinate with weather predictions for the regional farmers and thus may be a little "iffy." Navigating the Tombigbee can be a little problematical also because, as they warn you, the charts are not to be used for navigation or weren't when we made the trip. When using this waterway, one also must be aware the tugs, all seemingly with large numbers of barges in tow, have right-of-way, so take care.

It must be remembered that travelling by personal water craft offshore can be somewhat dangerous for other reasons. Because of the drug operations constantly taking place in these waters, plus the occasional piracy, a traveler must be prepared for the uncommon-but-not-impossible encounter. We had installed an alarm system that we could set when retiring that would detect any sizeable approaching body and were quite well armed, each with pistols, rifles, and shotguns with sufficient ammunition to fight a short war.

Apropos this matter. While we were ashore during a stay at a marina in Grand Bahama, someone had stolen our St. Pete burgee (a small pennant designating your home club). We ordered another via sea phone to pick up at our next port. Upon arriving in local waters, we were stopped by the coast guard. They came aboard to search our vessel because our transmission had sounded very much like a rouse that could be used by the drug cartels to announce a shipment. They discovered no drugs, of course, but had questions about the armament. While producing our government firearms permits, one of the officers was examining my PPK. Upon leaving, he had "forgotten to return the weapon." Neither Kit nor I had it, so I radioed immediately. The vessel returned to embarrassedly deliver the weapon, but the amazing part of the performance was that the helmsman moved close enough that the officer could hand the weapon to me personally while maintaining the two boats arm's length apart in an open sea without either boat being touched by the other.

Recall of these occurrences are set forth as a reminder for any prospective boater to provide a few examples of the dangers of the activity and the fact that, especially in long-range cruising, it is imperative to respect the water and always to be aware that unusual and unexpected events can occur at any moment. *And* unfortunately, if these matters are not enough, you can always count upon yourself to do something dumb.

We were passing through a set of locks on our "big wheel" cruise that necessitated lowering the boats several feet to the new level. Kit was handling the forward lines dropped from the dock worker, while I took care of the stern. Suddenly, the phone rang in the salon. I threw my line around the cleat and ran into the salon to retrieve the phone. It was from Philippe (Woog International) regarding a set of statistics received from an investigator who had done a study for him. I said I would return the call shortly and ran back to grab the line. Regrettably, I had thrown the line around the cleat incorrectly and I was not able to remove it. It began tightening and maintaining the stern steady as the rest of the vessel continued its downward movement. With no alternative, I drew my knife, slashed the line free, tied a square knot to reattach the two pieces, and was able to continue our descent on a level keel. With a huge sigh of relief, a disastrous result caused by a really stupid mistake was avoided with only, I assume, questionable thoughts by the dock worker when he retrieved the lines after the boats departures.

So to reiterate, as long as you remember how important it is to be aware at all times of the possibilities for dangerous occurrences appearing at any time, you will be able to experience many days, weeks, and even months of enjoyable activity and a complete freedom unlike any other you can imagine.

A final note with respect to boating: I mentioned earlier about our carrying a motorcycle aboard for local transportation. If you enjoy golfing, tennis, or other, it is wise to carry the necessary equipment with you because of the many opportunities that a traveler finds after docking on these trips. And not wishing to sound facetious, and depending on your personal tastes, it is worthwhile to carry formal attire aboard. We were able to dine at the yacht club's dining room upon docking on three occasions because they were having a strictly formal dinner for club members only—two were the club's commodore's ball, where each one was even gracious enough to invite us to sit at his table. The third was at Cooper Island in the Caribbean, an upscale port that offered superb dining and, if desired, overnight accommodation for persons willing to pay three thousand dollars per night for a condominium with swimming pool, personal maid, and breakfast. So boating also provides a peek at, and entrée to, another world if desired.

CHAPTER 9
Golf and Associated Activities

As most business men and women are fully aware, golf provides and constantly is used as an excellent venue for conducting business in a more relaxing fashion than provided by offices or stuffy boardrooms. Opportunities today are numerous. This practice began to develop and rise to a position of prominence in 1900s. Not immune to its value, I relied upon it many times and in the earlier days found it an excellent means of obtaining exercise as well. As time progressed, carts became a must, however, and today, they are mandatory on most courses because as with all of modern life, even a round of golf for supposed relaxation must be accomplished "in a hurry" rather than as described by the old adage where one should remember: "Don't worry, don't hurry and take time to smell the roses."

Which brings to mind a pertinent aside: check any bunch of roses today and you will discover almost invariably that roses today have been altered to remain in full bloom for considerably longer than previously, *but* no longer do they have an aroma. An advantage (?) has been set forth by the new era *for* the new era. Again, it depends upon your interpretation.

With respect to carts for playing golf. Obviously, it has removed golf from the realm of exercise and no doubt has helped to add to the problem of fat accumulation almost universally bemoaned by people today. Among our basic medical courses at Harvard was one in nutrition, its importance, and the need to include physical activity. They even provided us with a handbook of portion size and calorie count, which I retained for years. As a firm believer in doing what I tell others to do at a later time as an instructor, I always have maintained a high level of physical activity.

And I recall a fact that only is learned the hard way. Exercise actually is a relaxing activity as long as you select something you enjoy doing, *but* the moment it becomes necessary, the focus changes (e.g., early on, I found running several miles a day enjoyable until I began boxing for money). As a requirement, it became distasteful.

Sports other than golf eventually took its place and offered a large variety. Boating, just described at length, not infrequently requires large amounts of physical activity. My other personal selections were swimming, golfing, and tennis with occasional running if nothing else was available at the time. Granted, the level of exercise has been greatly reduced, although I still swim or walk at least a half mile daily. Golf, with its nonsport use of golf carts, I attempt to avoid at all times possible, recalling another aside

Back in the early days when the Desert Inn in Las Vegas owned a golf course on the Strip, I went to the Pro Shop to see if I could play a round. He called my timing perfect because he had a threesome preparing to tee off (when rules called for foursomes only). The reason emerged as to why a threesome was being allowed to play as soon as I was introduced and welcomed into the foursome. It consisted of Dean Martin; Don Cherry, a less well-known crooner at the time; and a fourth, whose name I do not recall. It was an enjoyable round enhanced by the repartee between Martin and Cherry, who would not ride because of attempting to gain a spot on the professional golf circuit. It also provided me with an opportunity to walk while the other two rode.

Another incident that allowed Kit and me to walk was a total surprise because it was at Pebble Beach, California. They had just experienced a rain storm that necessitated closure of the course for one of the very few times this type of call had been necessary. Eventually, they did reopen, but no golf carts were to be used. So we were able to walk the course, an experience few nonpro golfers can claim. Similarly, we were able to walk at Mahogany Run in St. Thomas in the Virgin Islands because the rental cart had defective brakes that failed, giving us some tense moments on a rather steep path negotiating a turn overlooking a considerable drop. We walked the last fourteen holes, told the pro shop operators what had happened and where they could get their cart. Apologies were offered and money completely refunded. We were pleased to accept the return of expenses even though we had enjoyed the walk. Unfortunately the course now is in a bad state of repair following the last hurricane. It now is closed and for sale.

The golf courses we have played through the years on trips taken strictly for that purpose, as well as those taken for other reasons, have been numerous and highly varied in nature and especially in foreign countries. Carts are forbidden or optional with most golfers declining because they would be stuck with players who were walking. The courses also offered golfing greens ranging from oiled sand to various types of grass, each of which offers its own characteristics to change how one's ball will roll toward the hole. Further, participation ranged from "fun" rounds to pro-amateurs (pro-ams) and other competitive tournaments both here and through large sections of the world, including Saudi Arabia, Morocco, Japan, Egypt, Israel, England, Scotland, and Switzerland, many quite "famous."

- Troon in Scotland we played before it was awarded the honor of becoming Royal Troon.
- Valderrama, Spain, home of the Ryder Cup in '97.
- World Amateur Championship played in 1982 in Lausanne, Switzerland, under auspices of the International Golf Federation.
- Royal St. Georges, where we played the course two weeks before the British Open was held (and thus extremely unusual) as a courtesy by the owner of the hotel at which we were staying, a man whose name ashamedly I cannot recall, especially when, in addition to the courtesy of playing the course, he gave me a monogramed tie, which I still have in my possession.
- Dar es Salaam in Morocco, where the king, who was an avid golfer, held an invitational tournament yearly until being shot at. He stopped the tournaments and built himself a smaller course within the palace grounds. Friends have not believed I naively had sent him a complementary note on the course. I did—a large tray of assorted fruits appeared in

our hotel room—and when we checked out, our bill had been paid.

- Famous Balleybunion and Lahinch courses in Ireland, and numerous others there and in the other countries that bring to mind so many additional memories.

In Spain, besides Valderrama, we played a large number and variety of courses because we frequently visited our small villa on the water in Marbella, a short way from Puerto Banús with its accompanying fabulous shops of designer clothing, shoes, jewelry, and more, which where most appealing to the occupants of the large number of internationally owned yachts that visit and often stay for the winter months. The small town Mijas is close to the port as well as our casita. It has a pleasant golf course, which we often played if not wishing to drive any distance. We were joined for rounds several times by the actor Sean Connery, most remembered for his roles in the Ian Fleming's movies as James Bond, the international English spy 007 character who preferred his martinis shaken but not stirred. He owned a small villa there and was a most charming individual with numerous fascinating tales about many things.

Kit and I also were fortunate in being able to collect a considerable number of trophies in various tournaments. Quite a number of club championships, but also a sizeable number while members of the National Senior Golf Association (NSGA) where we played within the United States courses such as Coeur D'Alene, Pinehurst, Sawgrass, Las Vegas courses, and more, as well as numerous in Portugal, Spain, and other European countries. On our own, we played a large number in Hawaii, including the Mazda International, in which I won the senior championship, and Kit took the foursome title with three friends who were members of the Arnold Palmer course in Orlando.

One more aside with respect to Bay Hill (Palmer's home course). We had no children and appreciated the offers to spend time with others on Christmas and the associated holiday season but felt like fifth wheels when joining family groups. So Kit and I usually traveled somewhere. One of our trips was to the relatively close Bay Hill Country Club in Orlando. As we were the only ones seated in the dining room when Arnold Palmer, his wife Winnie, and two guests entered, he said, "Good evening," and proceeded to their table. Shortly thereafter, a waiter approached and asked if we were alone, and if so, Mr. Palmer asked if we would like to join his party. Obviously, we said yes and were moved to their table. I was never particularly impressed with Palmer for some unfathomable reason but found the man to be a very gracious host and a thoroughly enjoyable conversationalist.

But enough of golf, except for mentioning one other unique course we visited but unfortunately did not play. It is the last course in the world before entering the waters of the Antarctic just outside the town of Ushuaia (pronounced Uh-sh-ayi-ah) on one of numerous cruises we have enjoyed taking when not otherwise occupied. This one followed the old route taken by the sailing ships from San Francisco down the coast "Around the Horn" and with a short sojourn at the Falkland Islands before terminating at Buenos Aires to fly home. And I did buy a gold earring to wear in my right ear apropos the tale that every seaman who made a successful trip "Around the Horn" wore with pride. And, yes, I actually did wear it for some time receiving numerous remarks of varied nature.

CHAPTER 10
Shooting Sports

Early in the book, I reported my introduction to the use of firearms and the many trips with my father on hunting and fishing trips. Once I reached the age where I began to experience the physical decline that accompanies the process, I realized my golfing days were over. I had begun playing when wooden clubs were still used, and my first set was made of this material. After experiencing the advantage of steel shafts and the increased distances that could be obtained, a switch quickly ensued with thorough enjoyment of the results. With the advent of age-related changes, however, I discovered that the added ability offered even by these clubs was insufficient for me to keep up with the new opponents I was facing. Admittedly, my ego came into play forcing me to move to other pastimes. I returned to the "toys" of my youth. Goose and duck gunning are highly enjoyable sports indulged in by many and great opportunities are offered by the seasonal migration of Canada geese down the eastern flyway with a concentration taking place in the Chesapeake Bay area. Shooting these birds in this area has acquired almost ritualistic status through the years but also has changed. You usually asked the farmer if you could shoot on his land and were rewarded with an okay often accompanied with a request for one or two of the birds for compensation. Gradually, professionals have convinced the farmers, for a fee, to be allowed to build bird blinds. During the season, prospective bird gunners pay the guides for their use. They usually accompany you so they can "call in" the birds. They do so by manipulating a small unit you blow through to produce calls that attract the flying birds to drop down and visit with the decoys, which have been placed strategically in front of your blind. It is possible to act as your own guide if you are familiar enough with the variety of calls needed. We were able to do so occasionally because of my early days of practice with my father when you asked the farmer for permission. Kit became an excellent gunner and during the season we often had enough to have guests for dinner. Wild goose meat has a unique taste totally unlike that of farm raised or store-bought birds. One obvious reason is that there is no fat. These birds fly for miles and when in the water constantly are swimming and diving. The strong "wild" taste, to which many object incidentally, can be removed or greatly reduced by roasting in beer.

The hardest part of preparing geese for the table is the cleaning and apropos my father's strict code with game of any type: "If you catch or kill it, you clean and eat it!" As an aside, one must be careful in eating wild birds. Some of the shotgun pellets responsible for downing them are in the meat and can be quite damaging if not being careful in how much pressure you apply when first biting down on a portion.

Two occurrences associated with our quest for wild geese may be amusing. When preparing to hunt, shooters meet their guides in a particular restaurant of the guides' choice and order breakfast. They are healthful meals that include large amounts of meat and other servings that were referred to as "food that would stick to your ribs." The time is around 4:00 to 5:00 a.m. because you must eat, get picked up by your guide who is sitting with the others, and drive to where the blind is situated. The first time I introduced Kit to the sport was in the days she wore her hair long, as was the style, and we both wore newly purchased hunting clothes—she was new to the sport and mine long ago had disappeared. Breakfast completed, the guides began gathering their shooters and departing until one was left and us. He finally got up, came over, and dispiritedly said, "Well, I guess you're with me." His attitude said it all: "Why me? Here's a guy who doesn't know his butt from his elbow who brought his good-looking secretary or whatever out to pass the day, and I'll be lucky if they don't shoot me." About thirty minutes after we arrived at the blind, a sizable toll of geese flew over. We both dropped our limit of birds, and we were the first of the groups to return to the restaurant for hot coffee (it often can be very cold and was that morning). We returned to that particular restaurant several more times, as well as in subsequent years, because of its general popularity. We also discovered we were "famous" among the guides, "the odd couple who performed so miraculously the first day of the hunt."

The second incident was a trip to hunt followed by a dinner being held at a hotel in Washington D.C. by Colgate to introduce Arthur Godfrey, a very popular entertainer of that time, as the new celebrity "face" for the company. We finished our day of gunning, drove to the hotel with the birds in an ice chest in the back, dressed for dinner, and had a pleasant evening with enjoyable company.

Other shooting sports enjoyed were skeet and trap, both indulged in by many and competitively as much fun as golf. Shortly after becoming comfortable back in this area, we were introduced to the Single Action Shooting Society (SASS). Established by a small group of men and women in the southwestern part of the United States, the sport spread rapidly because there seemed to be a certain nostalgia that had developed at that time in many of the middle age group. Presumably, a result of increase in pressure from the faster pace of life that had begun enveloping a large number of people who were conducting any type of business. Joining the organization was easy. You were required to select an alias that must be different than anyone else (verified from SASS records), assume the name, and dress in accord with your alias when attending functions and competing, and you must use only single action weapons. These either were the old musket of rifle similar to those used by the American frontiersmen, mountain men, and similar; a shotgun of similar capabilities; and handguns such as those used by the cowboy, gaucho, or Vaccaro—a gun that was loaded by black powder and/or cartridge that could only fire repetitive rounds by reloading after each shot was fired. Names accepted by the society's governors emerged as Muscat Rambler, Tex, Cat Ballou, Judge Roy L. Bean (the man I spoke about in the "Sculpture" chapter), El Tigre Viejo (name of an older Spanish caballero assumed by me), Kit as a smaller version of another cat La Gatita, and similar. Competition was held by assignment of shooters into manageably sized groups who moved from station to station to fire live ammunition at stationary or moving targets set up in different scenarios (e.g., defending an attack on a stagecoach, bank, ranch corral, fort and similar). A person accompanied the shooter through each course with a timer that starts with the first shot and is stopped with the last. And no, SASS never has experienced an injury from a gunshot other than a rare incident reported about an overanxious competitor literally shooting himself in the foot. If a shooter should for any reason drop a gun, he/she immediately is disqualified from continuing in any further competition. The organization has established strict rules of how to handle weapons at all times and has a range officer at each competition, whose word is law. It also is the reason for appointing well-trained instructors in advanced safety procedures as described earlier. Most of these individuals, like me, are or were NRA qualified.

We were introduced to SASS at a time when membership had grown rapidly to some eighty thousand plus and was expanding throughout the States and a short time later to European countries and Hawaii. Quite competitive in sports, we both acquired a number of awards including gold medals in the Huntsman World Senior Games for sportsmen over the age of sixty throughout the world. The Olympic-like competitions were held yearly in St. George, Utah, and besides shooters had participants in track and field, tennis, baseball, and several other sports. The three years we participated there were representatives from a surprisingly large number of countries, one I recall reported participants from thirty-two with as many as one thousand shooters. Competition consisted of assignment and competing in the usual manner but had added the "fast draw" competition that rapidly had been gaining followers. This competition is a replication of the old standard mano a mano face-off. Each twosome is lined up facing a man-sized target and at a signal, draws and fires a wax bullet as rapidly as possible toward the target situated seventeen feet away. The number of feet the bullet travels is from the average distance that has been determined from the number of confrontations that have occurred through the years in any exchange of gunfire between police and criminal or similar encounters. The target obviously must be struck to score, and the shortest time determines the winner. My usual times were not necessarily always the fastest (six seven tenths of one second with an occasional slightly faster time), but having read much about early gunfights and gunfighters, I followed movements they were reported to have favored and made sure I never missed. As time has progressed, I understand the winning time has dropped to the incredible time of fractionally under three tenths on a second. The last time we participated, I still won my gold at eighty-nine years of age.

But single action shooting sports too are succumbing to the modern individual's way of thinking. How many of today's younger generations have any interest in history? After all, the last American "gunfighter" was killed in 1918, and the last Indian uprising was a relatively mild resistance that occurred in Utah in 1923—all ancient history. The new breed of shooters now have forced the SASS powers to extend the weapons allowed to use replicas of the legendary Browning 1911 model automatic pistol in the various shooting scenarios, making it impossible for any single action weapon user to compete.

But now, I'm sure that any reader who has persisted this far has heard enough about this subject. It has entailed mentioning the NRA and instruments (tools?) that are legendary in this country and enjoyable for recreational purposes for a considerable segment of the population. Knowledge of their use also has saved lives as self-defense for persons I have known personally who live close to the border in Tucson. In spite of the antigun movement and the horror stories flooding the media, these individuals must live in country constantly invaded by drug traffickers and cartel rivalry. But for readers to whom this subject is abhorrent, I am sorry and agree wholeheartedly that the usual citizen has no need for bump stocks or even automatic weapons. My intent has been simply to attempt to show the enjoyable side of the sport even though they also soon may succumb to the increased pressure that will be placed on them by the purportedly coming action by the newly appointed administration, an administration that seemingly also ignores or possibly condones (?) taking a step that has brought problems to other countries that have initiated similar activities. But again, they seemingly support weakening the police force to the detriment of the law-abiding citizens of this country. However, I implore you; *please* to not place any political attachment to my statements. They merely are my straightforward evaluation of fact from my perspective.

CHAPTER 11
Some "Different" Trips

Numerous journeys already have been described. A couple more, memorable to us but not really belonging in the other areas, follow as of possible reader interest. One in particular began enjoyably suddenly evolved into a serious problem but ended with a remarkably acceptable solution. Still, this was only part way through a short journey that continued in a fascinating manner. We had decided to spend the Christmas/New Year period in our casita in Marbella. The flight went well; our stay celebrating with a few acquaintances at Puerto Banús quite pleasant; and even our decision to take a short ferry ride from Algeciras, Spain, to Ceuta, one of the small enclaves of Spanish-controlled territory in North Africa, was fun. We had decided to visit Casablanca again, and since we had rented a car when we had arrived in Spain from our usual agency, believed this to be most practical. The one hour plus aboard the ship was fine, but since it was New Year's Eve, we decided to stay overnight in nearby Tangiers. The next morning, we filled the tank with what we thought was gasoline and took off. We had not travelled too many miles before the engine began to malfunction. Arriving at a small village, we were fortunate to find a mechanic who informed us that the gas actually was gasohol, a mixture of gasoline and some type of oil. The gas station attendant either had been "hungover" or simply careless. Whatever, the mechanic said he could fix it but would need to drop and drain the entire system. Having no alternative, we said okay and moved into his cramped-but-adequate waiting room to wait with depressing anticipation of a huge bill when thinking of the monstrous charge we would get at home. Several hours later, we were on our way after being apologetically presented a bill for one hundred American dollars. Attempting to be sufficiently disgruntled, we paid him and once again were on our way. We drove to Casa Blanca and on our way back visited Fez and Marrakech. We also decided to make an overnight visit to what has become a tourists' mecca, the Casbah in Tangier. Much of the old city is drivable, thanks to action by the French during their occupation. Because the closely packed houses and maze-like streets that formed the Casbah had offered ideal conditions for armed resistance, the French army had razed houses, widened some streets, and actually bisected the area with a boulevard so they could move troops more readily. (Visitors always are afraid they'll get lost but you won't as long as you realize the quarter sits entirely on hills that spill down toward the sea. To get back to the seashore, one only has to keep moving downhill.) We stopped driving after a little while because I was not sure when drivable roads might run out and walking downhill to get out of the area is fine if you don't mind being forced to enter and move through a somewhat claustrophobic world without any hint of the sun and nothing but shadows and dust as you began the descent of a long, narrow ancient stone staircase about eight feet wide and enclosed by concrete-brick-mud buildings. Some structures with cantilevered overhanging portions extending well over the passageway almost to the building across from it. Descent along these paths most frequently are accompanied by a dominant odor of rotting fruit and decay. Then too, we didn't want to abandon a car, rented in a different country, with unpleasant possibilities that might possibly follow. Besides, driving was developing into a slow and difficult means of transportation because of the number of pedestrians. Men were leading braying donkeys or riding bicycles with baskets containing items ranging from small animals and loaves of bread, and heavily veiled women, often with dirty, ragged children by the hand, seemed to prefer walking in the middle of the road. At one point, there even was a bunch of youngsters playing soccer.

So although we did not find the infamous Café Detroit—remembered as the fabled visiting place of the writers, artists, and attendant expatriates of the 1960s—we did have dinner at a recommended "clean" restaurant. It offered a good array of dishes I have had, so we were relatively confident to begin. Included were...

- *Herita,* a thick savory soup usually served during Ramadan but often continued during the winter if the chef so decided.
- *Tajine,* a dish of beef cooked with olives and lemons or with prunes, quince, and almonds and served with couscous.
- *Tfaya*—chicken cooked with about every condiment you think of and, as usual, served with couscous.

- *Mechoui*—a lamb dish with a cumin spice combination pasted on the meat's surface before it is cooked.

They also featured Moroccan braised beef, I assume for the less adventuresome tourists. For dessert, we had the only Moroccan one I know, *Bastella*. This consists of alternate layers of thin crunchy paste, ground almonds, mashed pigeon, and is topped with sugar and cinnamon. The delicious dinner was consumed attended by only a small bit of accompanying trepidation after earlier observance of those open delivery carts that contained small live animals and long loaves of unwrapped bread.

Another unexpectedly memorable trip was because it included a typical *tourista*-oriented dinner at the Bunratty Castle in Ireland. As most dwellers in America, we had attended several similar productions within the US that feature jousting knights, wandering minstrels and maidens, and the rest. But this occurred during a business trip that was quite boring but finally finished. On a whim, we selected the dinner as something to do. The atmosphere was more authentic, as were the drinks and dinner, giving us an entire totally delightful evening. Nothing more to say really other than it provided relief from an otherwise difficult trip that no doubt proved enough of a stimulus to prepare us to become typical tourists for an evening.

A third journey, primarily for businesses purposes, left memories of varying proportions and variety. I had accepted a job of setting up a research project in South Korea, probably with a subconscious curiosity of what Seoul looked like after my remembrances of its wartime appearance in the '50s. After setting the project in motion, we had to fly down to Australia to check on the progress of a study that had been in progress for close to a year and pretty well wrapping up. While there, we again attempted to scuba dive the reef but were extremely disappointed. The area remaining for diving had been extremely limited and was the same allotted to snorkelers. Apparently, the restrictions had been imposed because divers, in typical *tourista* style, had been removing small sections of the concretions to take home as mementos. Such unseemly actions by persons who purportedly loved the natural wonders encountered in this world are almost too unimaginably difficult to absorb. But then again, the vagaries of human thought and action patterns when self-indulgence is involved long have been recognized. We decided not to undertake the activity, finished the business in hand, and headed out on the long trip back to Korea to assure all was well with the early phases of the study we had set in motion earlier. With more time available on our return to this country, it was possible to enjoy what had happened to the destruction and muddy roads remembered. Seoul had become a huge and vibrant city with huge apartment complexes lining the Han River similar to those lining the East River in New York City and areas replete with shop after shop featuring nothing but top-of-the-line designer offerings. The hotels provided none but the finest of amenities and service and entertainment that was most enjoyable. We flew home on Korean Airlines that also presented immaculate service and even gifted me a tie of my selection, one which I still have in my possession, although following today's relaxed dress code, rarely have cause to wear. But to summarize, it was an almost exhaustingly lengthy trip but one that furnished a wealth of memories.

Other journeys that supplied memories of a different nature were made to the Philippines, India, and Argentina. We had been invited to Manilla to represent the no-longer-present parents of the bride who was one of my technicians. Kit and I performed our duties in proper manner, wearing native clothing for which we had been fitted. Following the ceremony, we reacquainted ourselves with the city that I had visited in the war years. While strolling in a local park, a native man walking quite close to us was shot dead. It was a preelection period of one of Marcos's elections, and tempers were running high. The most sensible action for us appeared to be "get the hell out of there." We did on the next available flight and arrived home with quite mixed emotions.

In India, we had taken a short flight to New Delhi that arrived and set down in the midst of a riot, but most fortunately, we were extricated by a surprisingly discerning taxi driver, whom I commandeered to get us out of the chaos. He did, and again, we suffered nothing but some "white-knuckle" time.

A trip to Argentina was concluded, and we boarded the plane for home because it was a period that generated a large amount of unrest because the popular/unpopular Peron was returning to power. We no more than had gained altitude when an oil leak forced our return. We were to receive breakfast aboard, and since we had not, we were told to gather our luggage (another plane might be required for our flight to continue) and we would be taken to the airport's dining room. We did as we were told, but for our security, members of the military contingent assigned to the airport because of the tense situation were ordered to accompany us to and from the restaurant. Fortunately, we were able to finish breakfast, the plane's problem was discovered and corrected, and we resumed our flight. Peron's plane was beginning its descent as we dug for altitude and later read of "a small disturbance that had easily been taken care of when Peron had made his reentrance to the country."

Another experience that was not about the trip per se but rather the fascinating meeting we encountered while at our destination. While on a trip that included Egypt, we met Dr. and Mrs. Medansky at the Hilton for dinner. Shortly after being seated, a man entered with a sizeable retinue of heavily armed guards who spread throughout the room as this white-robed man was led to a nearby table accompanied by a lovely woman attired in a beautiful lace dress and wearing a diamond tiara that easily could be worth the proverbial "king's ransom." When our waiter approached, we inquired as to who this stunning couple might be. He said the man was ruler of the Emirates, and the woman was his wife, whom he had met while studying in England. She was born in Cairo, and he brought her home for her birthday every year. I told our attendant of the American custom of offering a drink to anyone celebrating such an occasion and asked that he inform them of my offer. They smiled, thanked us, and accepted a Coca-Cola. Later, as we were lingering over dinner with our usual extended conversation, they asked if we should like to join them for coffee and birthday cake. We did and spent a most enjoyable and memorable evening of conversation covering everything from sports to world conditions with two people who spoke impeccable English with a slight British accent. And for anyone wondering about the woman's dress, the Emirates long has been known as the most enlightened of the Middle Eastern countries.

But to finish on an even lighter note, I'd like to recount one that involves a charming couple from Holland. We were joined by Ana Marie and Morton, a couple who like ourselves were on a short golfing trip to Bermuda, where we were staying at the Princess Hotel. The round was enjoyable, and we extended our socializing with them for the remaining time on the island. The following year, we were in Portugal, staying at the Dona Filipa Hotel for a few days of golf during the Christmas holidays. We descended to the golf course after a leisurely breakfast, and who should we meet but Ana Marie and Morton, who were staying at the same hotel, accompanied by their two young adult children, whom they had brought along for the holidays. Again, a most enjoyable unexpected holiday season.

So again, to wrap up another section of our discussion, I hope these few occurrences will offer a quite simple but most pertinent aspect of extensive travel. Unusual and numerous almost diametrically opposing situations will be encountered if you do enough of it.

CHAPTER 12
Conclusion

Before beginning this wrap-up, I should like to remind the reader that I have said that repetition and redundancy would be avoided as much as possible when offering so many new and completely different pursuits that often include instances of the same or similar action. However, since this chapter deals almost exclusively with the generational differences, the quote from Hutchison seems worthy of recall since it so succinctly describes the mantra by which dwellers of my and many subsequent generations of at least the earlier 1900s were raised:

> We hope to be remembered as the products of a different country and society from which the United States of America has become in the last fifty years. Products of a far more disciplined society with rather rigid moral and social standards to which everyone was expected to conform given how society chastened and disciplined offenders. The way of the transgressor was hard. We were taught individual responsibility, that evil is due to character flaws in

the individual and not to the shortcomings of society.

Following the original quote, we briefly discussed the unnecessarily rigid confines set forth and acknowledged the need for modification. But upon again visiting the thoughts expressed, the need arises to take another look at some still relevant aspects. The tenets unquestionably established a basic moral code within each individual that he/she could decide if and where to institute changes. It too begs the question of whether later generations have failed to establish similar thoughts to be incorporated within the mind, conscience, or other pertinent area of the younger generations as time progressed. Consider today the almost totally corrupt jurisprudence department of the just barely *United* States of America. Think about the increasing calls of a pressing need to change the Constitution of the United States of America because of its long existence and thus attendant irrelevance because of age (?). Is *major* change truly necessary? Especially remembering that this document has held a nation together since its inception and ratification in 1789 with twelve amendments added two years later. So from 1791 to 2021, only adding thirteen more have been needed to further strengthen this masterfully written document to continue to guide this country successfully for 230 years. One also must consider what is rumored to require this process. A need to change the number of members of the supreme court after functioning brilliantly for so many years? Various changes in states' rights? Possibly. Amendments to guard against foreign intervention? Definitely with advent of computers. Security of electronic voting machines and other voter fraud activity? No brainer. Changes in the manner of police performance? Pause for thought! There is no doubt that many advances have been made in understanding the criminal mind and ways of treating the resulting aberrant reactions. Nevertheless, one also must remember that none of this material applies once criminal action is underway. The present overabundance of mob rioting repeatedly demonstrates the necessity for immediate action rather than discussion. When random looting and outright thievery, massive destruction of property begin and lives are threatened—even lost—some type of physical resistance and restraint must be provide *at that moment*. The time of analysis is past and totally irrelevant. Action is necessary *now* and more frequently than not, of a violent nature. Yet the administrative powers of several states are acting to reduce and even suggesting completely defunding of police departments irrespective of the fact that such reduction and/or abolishment simultaneously removes any viable means of protection for the individual citizen. The resulting situation at this beginning of 2021 is closely approaching anarchy. Witness the attack on congress. Additionally, legislation already is being considered (and reportedly already partially enacted) in some areas for release of criminals incarcerated for so-called "minor" crimes, many of which are reduced in the requirement for time spent in prison by renaming the crime already listed as ordinances with names designated as a crime requiring a longer period of incarceration. And almost beyond belief, these changes have become matters of *political* importance, a most devastatingly miserable and utterly disappointing wedding of elements that have no place whatsoever in any political agendas.

And then we are confronted with the racism issue that has existed in this country from its earliest import of persons from other parts of the world. Persons unacquainted with history may not even realize that many of the earliest destitute members of European countries unwittingly committed themselves to virtual bondage by becoming indentured servants. Wealthy farmers and businessmen in America would provide for the passage of these unfortunates with the understanding that upon their arrival they would work for various periods of time that often were extended for many years with no or minimal recompense. The term of employment frequently was extended by the ploy of allowing them to purchase necessary but otherwise difficult to obtain items from the employer on credit.

And then there is the "Black Lives Matter" movement. And make no mistake. Black lives *do* matter, but as already discussed, so do the lives of Chinese, Vietnamese, and other minor Asian groups, as well as Jews and Europeans, whose lives they are destroying when their frequent "peaceful marches" often turn into chaotically destructive affairs, where the more criminally inclined element destroy and burn buildings after looting them while fighting and injuring the often few police who are greatly restricted by their superiors in how aggressively they can attempt to control the situations.

Additionally, there is the growing appeal for restitution for all persons of African descent because, unlike other nationalities, the residents of the US in large part are descendants of men and women captured and brought here to be sold into bondage, where many even suffered more degradation and heartache with splitting of their family group by being sold to different owners. A completely abhorrent picture that still exists in parts of Africa and some of the Muslim world and in many ways can be compared with the frightening amount of sex trafficking that reputedly is crossing our borders and even worse, when billionaires such as Jeffrey Epstein could be found culpable and imprisoned as one of the perpetrators

Still, there is no reason why the possibility of restitution should not advance *but* with care. It must be remembered that a sizeable number of men and women of color moved to America as free citizens after successful revolts in their native island countries and that a number of blacks themselves were slave owners in the US. So to reiterate, the situation *definitely deserves* thoughtful consideration but through a process that must be thorough and without *any* political influence, which so aggressively is trying today to insert its influence in every activity possible. Additionally, discussion of this subject, as well as numerous others, needs a return of the media to reporting what really is going on.

Dependent upon how much one can believe material gathered from TV and the Internet, there is another aspect of the position of black residents of this country. From interviews of highly respected members of several "think tanks" and a few ministers of religion, part of the problem with the seeming ability of black citizens to rise in employment and accompanying social position results from the message they constantly hear. These respected individuals unanimously agree that much—if not the entire—cause of the problem is highly influenced by the message repetitiously given in the sermons of the black pastors, one that stresses the requirement of restitution and the need to provide help for this race that has been so poorly treated for so many years. Such a message, oft repeated, serves to solidify and even deepen the distress of the person already carrying a large amount of anxiety, lack of confidence, and even self-hate. And then, it might be wise for these pastors to remember the final plight of the original inhabitants of what became the United States. The American Indian suffered severely when depending on largesse of the governing body similar to that in the minds of many advocates.

It also must be remembered that each group of new arrivals to America—the Germans, Italians, and other Europeans, as well as arrivals from Asians countries—have had to struggle to survive and climb to a higher stratum of society. Granted, they arrived because they had wanted to come rather than arriving to be sold into slavery. But Blacks were emancipated by the Civil War and, with the advent of members like Martin Luther King, had made great progress that only began to backslide with recent increase in unrest among the younger generations. And yet it may be asked if these cries for compensation can be completely justified for some of these younger men and women. And before you scream and take umbrage with this statement, *stop to think* for a moment. Consider the number of persons of tremendous attainment within the race beyond the many millionaire black athletes whose rise in stature stem from a physical ability, although even this has been developed by hard work rather than sitting and bemoaning the abominable treatment of their forebears. There are numerous others who have used their desire to ascend in their environment through using their minds. Recall Herman Cain, the former CEO who rose from poverty in the segregated south to this position for a highly successful pizza chain and a candidate for president of this country; John Conyers Jr., the longest serving Democratic congressman, who just passed away at ninety years of age; four-star general and former secretary of state, Colin Powell; Condoleezza Rice, also secretary of state (under George W. Bush); Dr. Ben Carson, a pioneer of distinction in neurosurgery and former presidential candidate raised by a single mother in Detroit and presently secretary of Housing and Urban Development. These are but a few prominent members of the race who adopted the mantra of individual responsibility and self-dependence for advancement in life. Dr. Carson also has provided two more interesting and most pertinent thoughts. He tells of he and his brother's disinterest in school and their constant attention to TV programs while his mother, whom he did know was illiterate, had noticed the great emphasis that the wealthy people, for whom she did housework, placed upon books. She came home, pulled the TV plug, and dictated that the boys begin reading two books per week and writing reviews. It was the beginning of the young men's reversal in attitude. The other by this man, a statement about the situation in the country, "where we dissect everything and try to ascribe some nefarious notion to it." We've reached a point in our society when it's time to grow up.

But I'm sure we have set forth far more than most readers wish to wade through and probably are wondering what they actually had bargained for in picking up and even progressing this far in this regrettably gradually expanding tome. However, just having observed the 2020 Christmas and 2021 New Year occurrences and wanting to leave on a lighter note, I should like to offer one more topic that cries for comparison between present-day celebrations and those of most of the last century. While perusing my old articles to weed out stuff—an irksome but necessary task performed occasionally—I discovered a piece which, to me, still is most relevant. The time was Christmas season, and I was a little sad after reading an article in the Tampa Bay newspaper and sent a letter to the editor that expressed my difference of opinion with those he had expressed. I think some of you might enjoy or at least gain pause for giving some thought to those it conjured up for me.

For some vague reason Christmas this year (2016) did not seem to be the vibrant time it has provided in other years. I do not know if this "feeling' belonged strictly to me or whether others felt the same. However, for me at least, a reason for its source finally seemed to have evolved.

In the Sunday, 18 December Tampa Bay Times, Jay Cridlin, the "Tampa pop music/culture critic" wrote an article entitled: "Your whining is not music to our ears." It begins "Oh, holy night, do folks love bad Christmas songs" and continues: "Each December, we collectively re-enter this cycle of kvetching and kvelling about the same old holiday songs, over and over until our brains are figging pudding." He provides samples—the songs we all, or perhaps some of us, know—Silent Night, Adeste Fideles, Chestnuts Roasting on a Fire, The Little Drummer Boy or perhaps the later popular Rudolf, The Red-Nosed Reindeer.

His article was well-written and certainly set forth his thoughts about celebrating the Yuletide in song and there is little doubt that most of today's readers will heartily concur with his assessment. Also, it is granted that we all have experienced some boredom at times with their repetitive rendition, but perhaps unfortunately, I must take exception to his stance. To do so, I momentarily must digress to provide brief qualifications for disagreement. I studied piano for several years, have loved all forms of music and enjoyed performances ranging from Arthur Rubinstein and Sergei Rachmaninoff to modern music performers Nat 'King' Cole, Oscar Peterson, the Beatles, Elvis, and the rest.

But to return, I believe Cridlin expressed quite beautifully and succinctly the attitude that prevails today not only with respect to music, but to life itself. We are a product of today's mores where survival is dictated by the pace. No one dines anymore. They eat while finding it necessary to accept every call, twitter or text. Pleasure is "fitted in' to one's work. The bottom line demands it. Thus, whether work- or play-related, life is frenetic, everyone knows the price of everything, but the value of nothing and the bottom line is the new God.

Obviously, our music must reflect our life style. It must be fast, it must be loud, almost all words must be largely unintelligible and or repetitious, and it does not matter as long as it has, and seemingly *must* have, an aggressive repetitive (jungle?) beat. And preferably, it must be provided as a musical 'production' number.

It is a sad commentary on music, as well as life in general, that any evidence of sentimentality must be eliminated at all costs. Even the faintest hint of this emotion must be avoided because it too has become politically incorrect. Not only has it been discarded from Christmas, but old favorites such as "One for my baby, and one more for the road," or "I left my heart in San Francisco" now are ancient and depict an emotion that as stated, in itself is politically incorrect and no longer should be allowed to exist. Perhaps, *if* one gives it some thought, the outrageous increase in killings, road rage, bullying, suicide rates, drug addiction and the rest may be quite understandable? Conceivably, could it be time to step back and reconsider that ancient adage provided earlier pertaining to roses and what today's science has done? But there is no doubt that Cridlin's thoughts and suggestions are those most compatible with those of most of today's society. The few carols I heard performed this year were highly 'personalized' versions little resembling the familiar Christmas tunes—similar presentations incidentally to many highly personalized renditions of the National Anthem that set forth none of the striking features provided by the written words. And with sad acceptance in many ways, I realized we were only producing more of the same type of listeners when I saw the wild reactions of the children to the jazzed up versions they we're observing in the Disney Christmas show and similar.

But, to conclude, I don't know how many might possibly had seen NBC's birthday celebration for Tony Bennet at the time, but it was for a man who most likely epitomizes today's mantra for survival that can be summed up in three words—Adapt or Disappear.

Many will believe my observations to be a regression. Admittedly, it has been written by an old dinosaur from a far-removed generation who began using computers when the publisher of his third text requested that manuscripts be forwarded only after assembly on a 'word processor.' Now a computer, admittedly I still grind out 2–3 book reviews/week, send e-mails, and have used Twitter and texting but with nothing that pressingly important, they are not part of my regular armamentarium. I also have not yet disappeared. So I guess it is possible that, like Tony Bennet, I somehow have accomplished the ability to Adapt.

CLOSING REMARKS

A few summarizing remarks, not really part of the largely descriptive material set forth, might furnish a little more with respect to the century differences.

The life of TV, spawned during the 1900s and as we know it, gradually is ending, although parenthetically, I'm not too sure that is so bad. At one time, it was called "the great wasteland." Now, the level to which it has fallen is an insult to even a normal level of intelligence and perhaps might be termed "the great intellectual morass." Regardless, the projected material is much easier viewed by hand held devices which can be viewed "on the run."

Desktop computers rapidly are becoming a "thing of the past." Telephones and iPads suffice and do it all more conveniently.

Quantum computers are on the way. The pressing need to handle the huge quantity of already collected reference data, as well as its ever-increasing amount, is necessitating this move. One of the leaders in the race is IBM, which already has an operational machine as well as experimental designs for personal models that purportedly will be operable within the next two to three years. Delay in the personal variety, probably because of the nature of quantum bits, so true individual models within this time frame are highly questionable for various reasons.

Enjoyable conversation, frequently associated with already diminishing "leisurely dining," will pretty much disappear. Increased marketing requirements and the advent of robots and AI soon will move the process along even more quickly.

Personal traits such as faith, love, loyalty, and empathy, already largely ignored by the millennials, will be rare to encounter.

And the winner? Of course, the increasingly all-important *"bottom line."* After all, such elements as increasing one's knowledge and retaining/developing the traits mentioned are unnecessary. As just reported recently, a young man earned 1.8 million dollars simply by besting other competitors in a regularly held tournament playing digital games. Hey, not bad, and at least he, unlike most millennials and following generations, will no longer have to be worried with their difficulties in attempting to write and/or converse, and they won't even have to wait until the robots do it for them. Spelling corrections and thesaurus suggestions already are incorporated in computers, and if further suggestions are wanted, there's always Google and similar.

Admittedly a most depressing scenario, but please remember that I have been part of a time in history that definitely has provided numerous horrendous situations: the Great Depression, the wars, the Holocaust, the Cold War, even the present-day chaotic world situation, not to mention the debacle taking place in Washington, DC and much of the rest of this country. Challenges even have emerged that upon occasion have called forth the reappearance of one's basic instinct just to survive. But then again, it also had been a time, at least until the later part of the century, when some of the greatest and most enjoyable experiences were available to all.

- Unrestricted travel with few of the often-lengthy delays encountered almost constantly today and none of the long check-in lines.
- Pleasant, efficient, nicely, and even courteously presented tasty meal service and acceptably attired travelers. Knowledgeable and helpful hotel employees and all of the amenities so often missing today.
- Symphony orchestras with excellent musicians and conductors; operas with renowned singers such as Dorothy Kirsten, Gladys Swarthout, Luciano Pavarotti, and Robert Merrill. Individual classical performers like Sergei Rachmaninoff and Itzhak Perlman, classical guitarist Andrés Segovia, and flamenco Carlos Montoya.
- Groups of musicians: Nat "King" Cole, Duke Ellington, Glen Miller, Tommy Dorsey, Cab Calloway. Popular performers whose words and songs could be heard distinctly and understood: Bing Crosby, Frank Sinatra, the younger Tony Bennett, Tom Jones, Elvis Presley, the Beatles. Individual performers Kay Starr, Oscar Peterson, Dorothy Donegan, Peggy Lee.
- The poignant songs performed by Fado singers in Portugal, the best of whom could actually bring chills to the patrons.
- And on and on ad infinitum.

Some small pockets, supported by a dwindling few still exist but increasingly are difficult to find because the great popularity no longer exists, and after all, it must be remembered that the bottom line calls the shots more than ever before.

Unexpected just occurring examples of generational differences.

Regrettably, further examples must be added to this increasingly distressing picture of the growing number of differences that have occurred in the last one hundred years.

The insurrectional-like attack on congress is regrettable and incredibly unacceptable and would have been unthinkable in the earlier generations by other than a deranged person. Today, obviously, more than a few such individuals exist.

Political affiliation has become a totally divisive and controlling factor in the previously *United* States of America. As enumerated earlier, riots repeatedly are occurring directed against government buildings and police departments in cities with reportedly only minimal attempts at restraint by the controlling Democrat party authorities. *Now*, the unsuccessful attack on Congress by the poorly thinking sympathizers of the incumbent Republican Party.

Cause: incredible interparty hatred. Almost unbelievably, the entire chaotic mess seemingly greatly stimulated, if not arising from, Donald Trump's defeating the believed-to-be-shoo-in president Hillary Clinton. Charges and counter charges are rampant and now has degenerated into the incoming Democratic regime, instead of completely familiarizing themselves and formatting ways of dealing with the gigantic problems facing the country, now spending a considerable amount of time on attempting to impeach the incumbent president one week before the end of his term. The charge(s) still are not agreed upon, similar to the first attempt to impeach that failed because of numerous erroneous ones set forth by the Democratic Party accusers. The present attempts may be more fruitful for political reasons because that party now controls both houses of Congress. But for purported continuation after he becomes a civilian?

Prominent no doubt, is the fact that much of the vitriolic activity against Trump started even before his inauguration. The man he was replacing, although having many of the faults exhibited by Trump and a controversial figure to some, had an ability to present the hopes and ideas of his party that they totally endorsed. By comparison, Trump was a typical successful businessman, whose personal traits, according to many disgruntled individuals, were totally unacceptable. He alienated all members of the Democratic Party, the UN, the news media, and even many members of his own party. To all appearances, the reason was because he attempted to run the country like a business and now made what he determined were decisions requiring action "good for the country" and for the "little guy." The controlling senate member Mitch McConnell even was filmed indicating that "Trump had a lot to learn about how political affairs were conducted," and the Republican speaker of the house exhibited almost total disregard. In other words, the belief is that decisions should be made only after talking the subject to death—viz, the impeachment debacle, a *sad* commentary that once again brings to mind the oft-repeated adage about "a camel being a horse designed by a committee."

Regardless, many of the man's accomplishments—record setting for several features of the economy; restraint of illegal aliens; action against China's movement toward world dominance; revitalization of the country's military power (all factually verifiable but seemingly unacceptable to a large number of contrary "personal" opinions by members of the opposing party and others *largely because* the man's personality has given rise to a huge amount of personal hatred that seems to be of almost insurmountable size). *Additionally detrimental* are the large number of undoubtedly poorly thought-out acts in which recently he has indulged, actions that could, and perhaps did, lead to horrendous consequences.

But still once more, and apologetically for readers uncomfortable because of the religious connotation to a very basic thought, "he that is without sin among you, let him cast the first stone" (John 8:7). We have provided numerous examples of the tremendously lowered appearance of empathy or understanding in the newer generations. However, who is so devoid of this emotion to be unable to comprehend such reaction as stemming from anger and mounting frustration resulting from more than four years of fighting for his beliefs with little to no support? Were his actions acceptable? *No!* The result? *Further division* in a country already divided to an almost inconceivable position. *And once again,* division in a manner *unthinkable during the last century,* and especially when the man's written and given speeches, as adjudged by individuals accepted as the most knowledgeable with respect to the country, show *no* seditious statements as defined by the Legal Information Institute and agreed with by others accepted as most knowledgeable on the Constitution.

Federal law against seditious conspiracy includes treason, rebellion, and similar offences can be found in Title 18 USC *ff* 2384:

Seditious Conspiracy and Federal Law: The Basics

The federal law against seditious conspiracy, as stated, can be found in Title 18 of the US Code (which includes treason, rebellion, and similar offenses), specifically 18 USC. § 2384. According to the statutory definition of sedition, it is a crime for two or more people within the jurisdiction of the United States:

- To conspire to overthrow or destroy by force the government of the United States or to level war against them;
- To oppose by force the authority of the United States government; to prevent, hinder, or delay by force the execution of any law of the United States; or
- To take, seize, or possess by force any property of the United States contrary to the authority thereof.

Free Speech, Sedition, and Treason

In order to get a conviction for seditious conspiracy, the government must prove that the defendant in fact conspired to use force. Simply advocating for the use of force is not the same thing and in most cases is protected as free speech under the First Amendment.

And *please*, once more, do *not* accuse me of taking sides politically. The subject has been one of considerable contention since 1798. Individuals readily may argue and turn the definition of sedition to their direction, and I have no desire to gainsay such action. My presentation simply is to present a description provided by a group of acceptably knowledgeable individuals along with the interpretation set forth by another group generally accepted to be authorities in interpretation of the constitution as written.

The political fallout? One hundred per cent confrontational and strictly to be avoided unless one may be willing to be alienated from a particular acquaintance(s) or even most recently reported from his political party. Thus, still another *huge* difference between members of the two eras. I was raised in a home where my father was a political "ward boss" for a number of years. He found it to be a diverting avocational way to relax. Further, discussions with acquaintances with opposing beliefs were enjoyable. Frequently, they reached a high level of intensity but were concluded without the seemingly continued lasting discomfort or even apparent hatred that occurs today. Fortunately, I too have found one person, Luis Costales, a nephew in Ecuador who espouses an ideology quite opposed to mine but exhibits an obvious level of mental acuity sufficient to argue strongly for his stance, and yet we can part sincere friends and repeat the performance when new features are encountered. But then again, single examples of what earlier generations simply referred to as "common sense." And we must be aware of the regrettable fact that previously, no one person has generated such intense personal animosity—a first in history.

Differences in era? Unmistakable examples of how early the degradation in empathy, understanding, and loyalty to this country began. Recall the words of Hillary Clinton, reaching adult status in 1967 and later, as Secretary of State, offered the infamously callous answer to congressional questioning about the embassy invasion that resulted not only in serious destruction of American property but several deaths including that of the ambassador who was tortured before being killed: "What difference does it make?"

And what about Mitch McConnell's recent (2021) statement that has the distinct possibility of aiding impetus toward moving this country from an ideology that for 232 years has provided a way of life that is seen as the mecca for less fortunate immigrants toward one that has not had a particularly good track record through history? The basic concept of socialism is one of the best there is. Regrettably, history shows that it *breaks down* because of the small amount of altruism existent in too sizeable a number of human beings. The Senate leader, because of his acknowledge power of persuasion, when asked his position with respect to removing the still-sitting president, his answer was an equivocal statement that it would require each person to search his conscious, an answer that did not affect a few lives—*instead,* those of an entire country. I rest my case: *quod erat demonstrandum.*

But to continue, I'd like to ask indulgence of you wonderful readers with enough tenacity of purpose to have pursued this far. The old dinosaur has one more observation that is only tangentially pertinent to our mention of common sense. A TV commercial has begun showing a man backing out of his driveway and being able to stop quickly from backing into a passing truck by use of an electronic device that senses the oncoming vehicle that he cannot see because bushes on both sides of his driveway. The technological advancement is commendable, but wouldn't common sense dictate that the man lower the height of the bushes so dependence upon the technology would not be required? Or if for some undeterminable reason the bushes could not be lowered, at least backing into his driveway would do much for lessening the problem. Such activity would be dictated by "common sense" such as employed by earlier generations.

Finally, however, honestly, *my closing remarks*. In answer to the more usually *unasked* but easily discerned question of what a guy this old can possibly still enjoy is simple: good food and wine leisurely enjoyed with scintillating conversation, good books, and continued participation in daily physical activity such as a swim (in a heated pool if necessary) or if too cold, a session on the treadmill and/or rowing machine. And yes, conversation can be enjoyed in spite of the continued restrictions required with advent of the corona virus. Kit and I thoroughly enjoy talking with each other as we did quite a number of years ago in the six-month cruise by ourselves described earlier, and Skype and Zoom present abundant opportunities for speaking with others. The end of 2020 and introduction to 2021 was celebrated by a Zoom connection set up by Michael Laredo (MOMO, the well-known Canadian guitarist and professional interviewer on Facebook) and his lovely wife, Crila; along with Matt Eichen, a former student of mine who retired early from a successful surgery practice to return to his earlier love of music, where he has established a highly successful guitar manufacturing business; his charming wife, Dawn; and their young adult son and daughter. The session began at 11:45 and continued until after 3:00 a.m. New Year's Day and continued (after 1:00 p.m. because the old guy needed some sleep) with several additional Skype conversations with other friends.

The second question that always *is* asked of course: "What do I believe to be the secret of living to be one hundred years old?" For me, the answer entails a few specifics but actually is quite simple. Have a sincere faith in God (or whomever you accept as the highest authority); inherit good genes; establish a good routine for nutrition, body and mind; believe in yourself but be totally honest (which may be very difficult upon occasion and calls for tough decisions); search for and discover one person with whom you can share mutual love and respect; set worthwhile goals and tenaciously pursue them, but remember to enjoy the obtainment as well as the pursuit; do not allow setbacks to confuse you but learn from them; be honest and trustworthy, and be considerate; think before you speak; and always remember: money is *not* the Holy Grail!

And while remembering all of that, make sure you think about the important words uttered by a popular entertainer of many years ago by (as I recall) a man named Hubie Smith. His lament: "If I knew I was going to live so long, I would have taken better care of myself."

So to sign off with still another's once-well-known famous words: "That's all, folks!"

ABOUT THE AUTHOR

The author has functioned simultaneously as a research scientist and pathology professor, world lecturer, textbook and award-winning fiction author, nationally/internationally recognized sculptor, US Coast Guard Merchant marine licensed captain and master who also has won national and international sports awards and served in WWII and the Korean War. Today, he reviews books for Amazon and occasional others on request. His web page is www.johnmanhold.com

Enriqueta (Kit), Manhold has degrees and/or certificates in pharmacy, fashion design and diesel engine maintenance and has been an intimate part of the last fifty years of this journey.

IMAGE GALLERY

Published in 1968

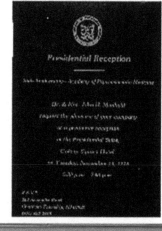

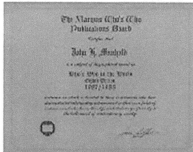

Early Years & Military

Chris Brent in
Peg O'My
Heart
1936

Captain
Stanhope in
Journey's End
February
28th 1936

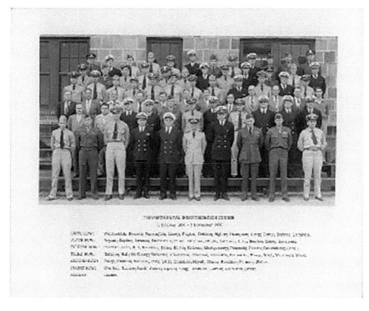

World War II & Korea

3 WWII retreads, Manhold, Maninan, and Kelso recalled and reporting in to camp Lejeun'n for upgraded marine combat training for Korean war. June 1951

Marine corps Headquarters personnel at Honolulu, Hawaii

𝔖cientist

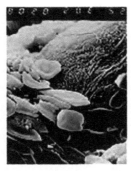

Edge of an open wound showing red blood cells that are dying but still viable enough to deliver oxygen to the underlying regenerating tissue.

Micro respirometer that measures amount of oxygen delivered (QO2) by 1 ml of wet weight tissue used to determine viability of above pictured cells. With later concurrently conducted psychological studies, we were able to determine further the extent to which mental conditions such as depression, tension and similar attitudes affected delivery of this vital element to aid wound healing.

Interesting aside:
Apparently I was the only one studying RBCs outside of the body which initiated an Invitation to Moscow's Academy of Sciences because they seem similarly to have been the solo investigators of white cells.
This is back in the 1950's when hyperbolic pressure was the all the rage in wound healing.

Micro Respirometer (assembled)

Micro Respirometer (disassembled)

Educator

Distinguished Harvard Alumni Award

𝔄𝔲𝔱𝔥𝔬𝔯

<u>Texts</u>

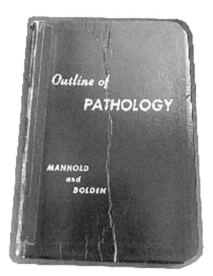

1960

1956

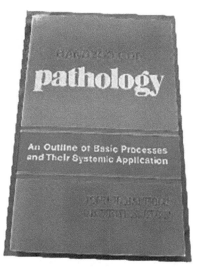

1987

Textbooks in other disciplines published; Clinical Oral Diagnosis 1965;
Psychology, 1984 and a lexicon in 4 languages in 1985.

Novels

Sculptor

"DAYS OF GLORY PAST"
Bronze
1st Copy
City of West Orange,
N.J.

2nd Copy
Farleigh
Dickinson Univ. N.J.

Barbados Image
African Wonder
Stone

"JACQUES PICCARD,
OCEANOGRAPHER"
Bronze
Piccard Collection,
Bern, Switzerland

"DNA"
Polished Bronze,
Sloan Kettering,
NYC

"TORSO"
Polished Bronze
1st Place, Paris,
France

3 copies in
Private Collections

"SEAHORSE"
Carved Alabaster
Private Collection

"JUDGE ROY L BEAN"
Founder of SASS

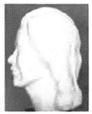

"KIKU YAMADA"
White composite
Wife of Isyotoru Yamada,
former executive, Toyota Motors,
Nagoya, Japan

Boating

Katita

48" Troller "Katita 2" delivered

"Katita 2" preparation

Golf

A few bag tags from around the world with a towel from Egypt

Shooting

Huntsman World Senior Games
2007

𝕿𝖗𝖆𝖛𝖊𝖑

Wedding in The Philippines

Manila airport, Leaving
early due to election uprisings

Locals pronounce it "Oh-Sh-Ayi-Ah"

Punta Loma Patagonia Argentina

Throwing Hawaiian lei overboards as custom when leaving

Royal Suva Yacht Club, FIJI

"Sweden is the off season "haul your own luggage"

On the "Around the Horn" trip

Using a map to seek for land to bute on Martaliu, Spain

Fanning for gold in Alaska

Landing in Helsinki Finland after flight from Russia, with hats from Gum's Department Store

Frank Shimasaki's General Merchandise, Pago Pago
in 1970's as it was in WWII

Pago Pago Yacht Club, American Samoa

158

Toys

"If you catch it or kill it,
you clean it and eat it"
-John Manhold Sr.

Gun cabinett
'Toys' of the trade